D0438723

Stewardship

Stewardship

Lessons Learned from the Lost Culture of Wall Street

John G. Taft

WILEY

John Wiley & Sons Inc.

Copyright © 2012 by John G. Taft. All rights reserved.

Published by John Wiley & Sons, Inc., Hoboken, New Jersey.
Published simultaneously in Canada.

No part of this publication may be reproduced, stored in a retrieval system, or transmitted in
any form or by any means, electronic, mechanical, photocopying, recording, scanning, or
otherwise, except as permitted under Section 107 or 108 of the 1976 United States
Copyright Act, without either the prior written permission of the Publisher, or authorization
through payment of the appropriate per-copy fee to the Copyright Clearance Center, Inc.,
222 Rosewood Drive, Danvers, MA 01923, (978) 750-8400, fax (978) 646-8600, or on
the Web at www.copyright.com. Requests to the Publisher for permission should be
addressed to the Permissions Department, John Wiley & Sons, Inc., 111 River Street,
Hoboken, NJ 07030, (201) 748-6011, fax (201) 748-6008, or online at www.wiley.com/
go/permissions.

Limit of Liability/Disclaimer of Warranty: While the publisher and author have used their
best efforts in preparing this book, they make no representations or warranties with respect to
the accuracy or completeness of the contents of this book and specifically disclaim any
implied warranties of merchantability or fitness for a particular purpose. No warranty may be
created or extended by sales representatives or written sales materials. The advice and
strategies contained herein may not be suitable for your situation. You should consult with a
professional where appropriate. Neither the publisher nor author shall be liable for any loss of
profit or any other commercial damages, including but not limited to special, incidental,
consequential, or other damages.

For general information on our other products and services or for technical support, please
contact our Customer Care Department within the United States at (800) 762-2974, outside
the United States at (317) 572-3993 or fax (317) 572-4002.

Wiley also publishes its books in a variety of electronic formats. Some content that appears in
print may not be available in electronic books. For more information about Wiley products,
visit our website at www.wiley.com.

Library of Congress Cataloging-in-Publication Data:

Taft, John G., 1954–
    Stewardship : lessons learned from the lost culture of Wall Street / John G. Taft.
      pages   cm
    Includes bibliographical references and index.
    ISBN 978-1-118-19019-7 (cloth); 978-1-118-22761-9 (ebk);
    978-1-118-23726-7 (ebk); 978-1-118-26524-6 (ebk)
      1. Financial services industry—Moral and ethical aspects.   I. Title.
  HG103.T34   2012
  174′.9332—dc23

                                          2011048532

Printed in the United States of America

10 9 8 7 6 5 4 3 2 1

To individual investors . . . and their faith in a better future

The author is donating all proceeds from this book to charity.

Information in this book regarding individual companies and the performance of the securities they issue is for illustrative purposes only, and is not intended as investment advice. Individuals should work with their financial advisors to develop investment strategies tailored to their own financial circumstances, rely on the most recent information available concerning prospective investments, and understand that past performance of investments does not guarantee future results.

Contents

Foreword

John C. Bogle

No one concerned about the role of our nation's financial system can afford to ignore John Taft's marvelous call for *Stewardship* in the culture of Wall Street, and indeed in our nation and in our society at large.

Right at the outset, the author defines precisely what he means:

> Leaving a Stewardship legacy requires that we see ourselves not just as individual actors in economic or social systems, but as members of communities. It also requires that we define our purpose not in terms of self-interest alone, of "what's in it for me?" but in terms of how we can serve others. Finally, our Stewardship legacy is defined not just by how we serve others during our lifetimes, but by the impact of our actions on generations into the future. (Taft, xiv)

As I read through John's compelling book, I couldn't help feeling the passion of a kindred spirit, over and over again. For example, the author rails against "Finance Run Amok: Selfishness Trumps

Stewardship" (Chapter 2). In my case, I rail against the Wall Street Casino, where salesmanship trumps stewardship; where marketing trumps management; and where the mutual fund industry—the field to which I've dedicated my entire 60-plus-year career—has changed from a business in which "we sell what we make" to one in which "we make what will sell."

What has developed in the world of finance can be aptly described as an *agency* problem, the classic conflict between agents and the principals who they are honor-bound to represent. This conflict is not new. In the Old Testament, Ezekiel 34 says, "Woe unto the shepherds of Israel, for they have fed themselves and not their flocks." In the New Testament, Matthew 4:3 and again in Mark 15:30 asserts, "No man can serve two masters."

It's all about what happens when agents ignore that principle, too often placing their own interests ahead of the interests of their principals. As Taft puts it,

> What drove this growth in the relative importance of financial firms and their simultaneous ability to generate historically outsized returns? Those returns were possible because financial institutions, particularly the larger ones, stopped acting merely as agents on behalf of their clients and started increasingly acting as principals on behalf of themselves . . . . creating a culture and set of values different from those of a firm dedicated to helping solve customer problems, facilitate customer orders, or meet customer needs. (Taft, 14)

Quoting Steven Young, author of *Moral Capitalism*, Taft reminds us:

> This concept of *agency*—which has embedded in it the concept of serving others—is the link between Stewardship principles and moral behavior. It is the corporate equivalent, if you will, of empathy . . . . A moral sense requires sensitivity to "the use of power when others come into view . . . . Moral responsibility is a form of stewardship, of agency, of fiduciary undertaking . . . . It is a vision of mutuality, of service, of both self and others." (Taft, 14)

In describing how our financial system has failed us, the author is not afraid to name names. And, while he can only scratch the surface without turning his book into a tome, name them he does, for example, Goldman Sachs, UBS, Merrill Lynch, and Reserve Fund. More broadly, a quotation from Paul Purcell, CEO of Milwaukee investment banking firm Robert W. Baird & Co. encapsulates how an entire industry went wrong:

> There's no question our industry has lost its way. Not just the big firms. But the bigger firms get, the more focused they seem to become on pushing proprietary products, on finding ways to make money on all sides of a transaction—structuring, selling, hedging, trading—to the detriment of their clients . . . . It's greed, glorious greed. (Taft, 34)

As I reflected on those words from John Taft's book, I quickly recalled a similar but even more stinging description of the failure of stewardship:

> I venture to assert that when the history of the financial era which has just drawn to a close comes to be written, most of its mistakes and its major faults will be ascribed to the failure to observe the fiduciary principle, the precept as old as holy writ, that "a man cannot serve two masters." No thinking man can believe that an economy built upon a business foundation can permanently endure without some loyalty to that principle. The separation of ownership from management, the development of the corporate structure so as to vest in small groups control over the resources of great numbers of small and uninformed investors, make imperative a fresh and active devotion to that principle if the modern world of business is to perform its proper function.
>
> Yet those who serve nominally as trustees, but relieved, by clever legal devices, from the obligation to protect those whose interests they purport to represent, corporate officers and directors who award to themselves huge bonuses from corporate funds without the assent or even the knowledge of their

stockholders . . . financial institutions which, in the infinite variety of their operations, consider only last, if at all, the interests of those who funds they command, suggest how far we have ignored the necessary implications of that principle. The loss and suffering inflicted on individuals, the harm done to a social order founded upon business and dependent upon its integrity, are incalculable.

You might think those words came from a contemporary book on the recent near-collapse of our financial system, the crash in our stock market, and the interlocking of interests among institutional money managers and managers of our giant publicly held corporations. They did not. In fact, the words were spoken in 1934 by Harlan Fiske Stone, justice of the U.S. Supreme Court (later the chief justice of the United States) and later that year published in *The Harvard Law Review*.

While 78 years have passed since Justice Stone aptly described what had gone wrong in the financial system, we haven't done much—if anything—to resolve the problems of finance. Ironically, the Glass-Steagall Act of 1934 did a noble job in separating investment banking from commercial banking, but was effectively repealed by gradual erosion during the 1990s. Even more poignantly to me, The Investment Company Act of 1940 demanded that the mutual fund managers place the interests of their fund shareholders ahead of their own (Section 1, Part B), a policy requirement that has nonetheless been almost universally ignored in the industry.

Taft proposes numerous remedies to fix the system and one can only hope—even pray—that these remedies are more successful than their failed predecessors. He has high hopes (higher than my own) for the implementation of the reforms proposed in the Dodd-Frank Financial Reform Act of 2010. And he suggests that U.S. policymakers learn from the experience of Canada, which was well-insulated from the crises endured by its neighbor to the south. (Chapter 4 is entitled "World's Safest Banking System: Canada, the New Switzerland.") But it will take a renewal of the *spirit* of stewardship to cleanse and refresh our financial system, one that must be built on (in my own opinion) a federal standard of fiduciary duty for investment advisers and money managers, with protecting the interests of their clients as their highest priority.

More than parenthetically, I should note that the author shares not only my human and ethical values, but my investment values as well. He holds "core beliefs and convictions about how the financial markets operate—like mean reversion, like the predictability of asset classes over long periods of time, like the value of diversification." (Taft, 106) If investors would begin their approach to their long-term strategy with those elemental concepts, they would serve themselves well.

A closing word. The author of *Stewardship* has the experience, the standing, the high character, and (I might add) the temerity to write this powerful book. He is an industry insider, having served as chairman of the Securities Industry and Financial Markets Association (SIFMA), which is composed of the investment industry's senior investment executives. He's also a successful banker and manager of other people's money, with a broad career encompassing key top positions in both the United States and Canada.

And he's, well, a Taft. A member of a family that includes some of the staunchest members of America's political establishment, including a president, a chief justice, a U.S. senator, and more importantly, a family that honors the highest traditions of public service. His grandfather, legendary U.S. senator Robert A. Taft, was known as Mr. Integrity, in John Kennedy's words (in *Profiles in Courage*), "who stuck fast to the basic principles in which he believed," no matter what the cost. (Taft, xiii) John Taft knows those traditions.

If you hold those same beliefs—that integrity and fiduciary duty and stewardship are the keys to a better financial system, a better society, and a better America—you'll love this book. If you don't yet hold those beliefs, I believe that you'll be persuaded by this book's powerful message. Now, let's all get out there and start to do something about it.

John C. Bogle
Founder, The Vanguard Group
Valley Forge, PA
January 4, 2012

Introduction

On October 5, 2009, the day before testifying for the first time to Congress, I visited the Robert A. Taft Memorial and Carillon in Washington, D.C. A ten-story bell tower located between the U.S. Capitol and Union Station, it is the only memorial to a member of Congress situated on the grounds of the U.S. Capitol. I was to testify on behalf of financial service firms in front of the House Financial Services Committee. The U.S. Congress was writing financial regulatory reform legislation and it wanted the viewpoint of the banks, broker-dealers, and asset management firms most affected.

I visit that memorial because Robert Taft is my grandfather. My grandfather had public service in his blood. He grew up in the White House, one of three children of U.S. President William Howard Taft (1909–1913), who was the only president to also serve as Chief Justice of the Supreme Court (1921–1930). He was the leader of the Republican Party in the United States Senate in the 1940s and early 1950s, earning him the unofficial title "Mr. Republican." His four sons included a congressman and senator from Ohio, a U.S. ambassador to Ireland, and a physicist (my father) who served as dean of Yale College. His grandchildren include senior administration officials in the Department of

Robert A. Taft Memorial and Carillon in Washington, D.C.
SOURCE: Architect of the Capitol.

Defense, NATO, the State Department and Department of Health and Human Services, and a two-term governor of Ohio. Standing in front of Robert Taft's statue, I am at once inspired and overwhelmed by the power of my family's legacy; by the Taft family sense of responsibility and obligation to serve; and by our family's commitment, generation after generation, to giving back to society.

Throughout his life, my grandfather set an example of being loyal to core principles, and exemplified the importance of locking one's moral compass onto a personal true north. In his case, true north was the principle of "Equal Justice Under Law." To him, those words were the foundation of a free society. They were important enough to compel him to speak out against what he believed to be a controversial example of everything that was contrary to this principle, which earned him a chapter in John F. Kennedy's book *Profiles in Courage* . . . and also cost him the Republican nomination for president in 1948 and 1952.

"Robert A. Taft," Kennedy wrote, was "a man who stuck fast to the basic principles in which he believed—and when those fundamental principles were at issue, not even the lure of the White House, or the possibilities of injuring his candidacy, could deter him from speaking out."[1]

"[H]e was more than a political leader, more than 'Mr. Republican.' He was also a Taft—and thus 'Mr. Integrity.'"[2]

Perhaps because of those visits to the Taft Memorial, perhaps because of my family's legacy, I have always believed in the importance of core principles. I believe that if you don't get them right, nothing else matters.

Conversely, if you do get them right, everything else falls into place.

The origins of this book lie in a speech and a white paper titled *Creating a Clear Path Forward*[*] which I wrote for our individual investor clients—and, quite frankly, our employees—during the height of the 2008–2009 financial crisis. At the time, I was searching for something I could say to comfort them while they were experiencing things many of them had never been through before, such as a 50 percent collapse in the value of their retirement savings. My words needed to reassure them while they were feeling emotions more extreme and primitive than they had ever felt in their adult lives, like fear, confusion, desperation, even despair.

It's particularly in times like a financial crisis that core principles matter. Core principles are the only solid ground under our feet when everything is, or seems to be, unstable.

The solid ground I discovered in writing *Creating a Clear Path Forward* was the realization that we have all been put on the earth for a reason: to leave the world a better place than we found it.

---

[*]See Appendix C.

Perhaps because of those visits to the Taft memorial, perhaps because of my family's legacy, I have always believed in the importance of core principles. I believe that if you don't get them right, nothing else matters.

That, in a nutshell, is our Stewardship responsibility, our Stewardship calling.

Leaving a Stewardship legacy requires that we see ourselves not just as individual actors in economic or social systems, but that we see ourselves as members of communities. It also requires that we define our purpose not in terms of self-interest alone, of "what's in it for me?," but in terms of how we can serve others. Finally, our Stewardship legacy is defined not just by how we serve others during our lifetimes, but by the impact of our actions on generations in the future.

Our collective willingness to live up to our Stewardship responsibilities will determine whether or not we repeat or abet future recurrences of the financial crisis of 2008–2009. It will also determine whether we prevent similar sustainability threats to society in areas like resource scarcity, climate change, population growth, fiscal policy, and income inequality.

It's not an exaggeration to say that our future literally depends on our willingness to think and act like responsible stewards.

Chapter 1

Core Principles

The Ground Beneath Our Feet

Serving our clients is our basic purpose. Service is the chief contributor to our growth and profitability.

—The late Harry C. "Bobby" Piper Jr.,
chairman of the regional brokerage firm
Piper Jaffray & Hopwood

Never has the ground under my feet felt as shaky as it did on September 16, 2008, when I received a call on my office phone telling me the Reserve Primary Fund—a money market fund—had broken the buck and, more significantly, had indefinitely suspended redemptions of its shares. This meant that investors in this money market fund could not withdraw their money. Since RBC Wealth Management's clients had invested in the Reserve Primary Fund, this situation had an enormous impact on the investors we represented, our advisors, and our firm.

Reserve's announcement was triggered by the fact that the Reserve's portfolio managers had purchased and still held in the portfolios of

Reserve's largest money market fund—the Reserve Primary Fund—commercial paper issued by Lehman Brothers Holdings on the weekend Lehman Brothers declared bankruptcy. Commercial paper is short-term debt used by companies to finance themselves day to day instead of borrowing money from a bank. It is normally a highly liquid market. But not in the case of a sudden bankruptcy. Overnight, the value of the Lehman Brothers commercial paper fell to $0, or close to $0.

The amount the Reserve Primary Fund held of these securities, namely the Lehman commercial paper, was so large—$785 million—that it could no longer afford to offer its investors $1 for each $1 they had invested in the Fund. This is why it is called *breaking the buck*. As rumors of the decline in the Reserve Primary Fund's value hit the markets, the Fund received requests from investors with billions of dollars in the Fund to get their money back—the mutual fund equivalent of a run on the bank. Rather than sell off portfolio securities in the worst market in recent history, the Fund's trustees elected to indefinitely suspend redemptions—the mutual fund equivalent of closing the teller windows and locking the doors to the bank.

RBC Wealth Management-U.S., the firm I run, had recently acquired a well-regarded regional brokerage firm, Ferris, Baker Watts, based in Baltimore and Washington, D.C. Ferris, Baker Watts used the Reserve Primary Fund as the investment vehicle for its clients, as the place it swept clients' cash into, and as a vehicle for their investing activities. Our clients assumed their money market fund investment could be converted into cash by the next day. Now that the Reserve Primary Fund had suspended redemptions of Fund shares for cash, our clients had no access to their cash. This meant, in many cases, that they had no way to settle pending securities purchases and therefore no way to trade their portfolios at a time of historic market volatility. No way to make minimum required distributions from retirement plans. No way to pay property taxes. No way to pay college tuition. It meant bounced checks and, for retirees, interruption of the cash flow distributions they were counting on to pay their day-to-day living expenses.

Global Crisis of Confidence

That day, and the days that followed, were marked by chaos and confusion. Hundreds of thousands of panicked clients called their advisors, who called their branch managers, who called our home office in Minneapolis asking what we were going to do to help them. Reserve Fund's management was missing in action, refusing to answer phone calls. Information about the extent of their crisis was incomplete and confusing.

Incredibly, given the relatively small size of the fund, $62 billion, the Reserve Primary Fund's failure triggered a global crisis of confidence in the short-term credit markets, which is mother's milk to many corporations. For several weeks, this created the very real possibility that even the largest, most creditworthy corporations might be unable to roll over their commercial paper borrowings and, therefore, would find themselves insolvent. Our clients and our employees watched in horror as their net worth evaporated in front of their eyes.

To make matters worse, our operations professionals told us our processing systems didn't know how to handle money market fund shares priced at anything other than $1.00 a share. Unpriced Reserve Primary Fund shares were like sugar in the gas tank, threatening to bring our back office to a grinding halt.

I remember thinking, "It's true . . . you never see the bullet that kills you."

I couldn't sleep. I felt like I was falling down an elevator shaft, trying to find some kind of emotional bottom, some kind of solid ground upon which I could operate.

I remember thinking, "It's true . . . you never see the bullet that kills you."

It was in writing my white paper *Creating a Clear Path Forward* for clients and employees that I found solid ground. I found it in the realization and conviction that my purpose, at that time of crisis, wasn't to worry about myself. It was to help others.

"The best things in life don't cost money," I wrote at the time. "True wealth lies in relationships. I've learned that the best way to make it through a crisis is to stop focusing on your own problems and start helping others with theirs."*

One day after the Reserve Primary Fund failed, with the support and backing of RBC, I announced to RBC Wealth Management clients who had cash in the Reserve Primary Fund that we would make them whole

*See Appendix C.

The best way to make it through a crisis is to stop focusing on your own problems and start helping others with theirs.

for any losses they incurred . . . up to three cents a share. This was more than enough, we believed, to cover the loss in value of the Lehman commercial paper. I also announced we would lend money to any client who faced a hardship cash shortage due to their cash being locked up in their Reserve Primary Fund holdings.

RBC's willingness to do the right thing for the clients of Ferris Baker Watts kept our wealth management franchise together and allowed us to build enormous long-term loyalty among our advisors and our clients.

Responding to the Reserve Primary Fund crisis reaffirmed for me that the principles of Stewardship are core principles. They are my personal true north.

Since then, my own personal definition of Stewardship has evolved from a narrow and somewhat technical definition—*the responsible management of that which has been entrusted to one's care.* My new, more expansive version has to do with leaving a legacy, which I call the Golden Rule of Stewardship—*leave the world better off than you found it*—and the more existential formulation—*your purpose on earth is, ultimately, about service to others.*

I have spent most of my career, more than three decades, in the financial services industry. I have been an investment banker, the CEO of a mutual fund company and an institutional asset management firm, the head of one of the largest wealth management firms in America and, most recently, chairman of the Securities Industry and Financial Markets Association (SIFMA), the trade association for U.S. brokerage and securities firms and asset managers. I believe very strongly that the financial services industry, is at its very core, all about the concept of Stewardship, and all about Stewardship values and responsibilities.

After all, the foundation of financial markets is public trust and confidence. The word *credit* is derived from the Latin word *credere*, which means "to trust." So trust should be the foundation of the financial services industry, whose mission it is to serve the needs of others—its clients. The industry does this by matching people who have capital—investors—with people who need or have opportunities to deploy capital—corporations, governments, public agencies, and nonprofit organizations. The financial services industry's challenge is doing so in a way that makes everyone a winner; so that everyone is better off than they would have been without the products, services, intellectual content, and capital of financial institutions.

A Foundation of Trust

I consider myself fortunate to have been exposed very early in my career to Stewardship values and to a Stewardship culture.

The first firm I worked for after graduating with a master's degree from the Yale School of Organization and Management was Piper Jaffray & Hopwood, a Minneapolis-based regional brokerage and investment banking boutique headed at the time by a patriarch named Harry C. ("Bobby") Piper Jr.

I remember being invited to Bobby Piper's office within a week of joining his firm as a completely inexperienced and junior invest-ment banking associate, where, for more than an hour, he asked me questions about my family, my personal interests, and what I'd studied in college. He did this not because it was a pro forma exercise with all new employees, but because he truly cared about each and every new member of his corporate family.

Near the end of his life, Bobby became deeply spiritual. He spent his final years creating a mission statement for Piper Jaffray that focused on service. In doing so, he defined service to others as the very purpose of his family's firm:

"We, the people who are Piper Jaffray & Hopwood, believe that serving our clients is our basic purpose. We believe service is the chief contributor to our growth and profitability."

Simple. Elegant. And, as I hope you will agree after reading this book, profoundly transformational.

Agents of Main Street

We continuously read about the growing concentration of the financial services industry around a handful of global and systemically important institutions. The 800-pound gorillas include the likes of J.P. Morgan, Bank of America, Goldman Sachs, Citigroup, Wells Fargo, and Morgan

Stanley. Yet the financial services industry is in fact made up of thousands of firms like Piper Jaffray, many of them small businesses. The vast majority of them are located outside of New York City, and have a lot more in common with Main Street than they do with Wall Street. These smaller firms were every bit as damaged by the financial crisis of 2008 and 2009 as other participants in the financial markets. These Piper Jaffrays operate close to their clients, are part of the communities in which their clients live and work, and conduct their businesses day in and day out consistent with the core principles of Stewardship.

"My dad always thought of this as a noble profession," Bobby Piper's son Tad told me. "A profession in which we were privileged to serve the world, for which we were admired. He felt we had a higher calling—to help individuals manage their wealth; corporations raise capital; governments build roads and schools."

Indeed, the financial services industry operates as a laboratory, a test environment, for the core principle of Stewardship. When financial services firms remain true to their mission and their purpose as agents and intermediaries, they help allocate capital efficiently and promote economic growth. When they stray from that mission, when they stop thinking of themselves as agents and start behaving like principals, when they stop serving clients and instead focus excessively on returns to shareholders, then no amount of legislation or regulation can prevent the kinds of excesses that brought us to the brink of worldwide financial collapse.

We have learned from financial services firms, what happens when Stewardship values prevail, and what happens when they don't.

This book shares the conclusions I have drawn from managing financial services firms and from serving in leadership positions in the financial services industry over the past 30 years. It makes some suggestions as to how we can rejuvenate a commitment to Stewardship, not only to make our financial system safer, sounder, and more secure; not only to rebuild public trust and confidence in the financial markets; but also to address other equally important challenges we face as individuals, as organizations, as communities, and as societies.

The financial services industry operates as a laboratory, a test environment, for the core principle of Stewardship.

■ ■ ■

Interlude
Learning from Failure:
Acquainted with Grief

One feature common to the many leadership books, ethics texts, management articles, and social commentary I read in writing this book is the tendency for their authors to underplay the fundamentally flawed nature of human character, to preach leadership lessons from the podium-of-never-having-made-a-(serious)-mistake.

In fact, precisely the opposite is true. Failure—the experience of having made mistakes—can be a deep source of Stewardship wisdom.

Consider an article in the *New York Times Magazine* on political judgment and the war in Iraq, by Michael Ignatieff, who went on to become the leader of the Liberal Party of Canada before being handed a crushing defeat in Canada's 2011 elections. Ignatieff writes about what people look for in a leader: "They must be men of sorrow acquainted with grief, as the prophet Isaiah says, men and women who have not led charmed lives, who understand us as we really are, [yet] who have never given up hope . . . ."[1]

"Learning from failure matters as much as exploiting success," Ignatieff writes.[2]

Like most people, I have experienced Stewardship failure in my life. In my case, it happened more in my personal life than in my professional life, when my lack of emotional courage led, not in a straight line, but ultimately contributed, to the breaking up of my family and to my estrangement for several years from my three children, from which we are slowly, to varying degrees, working our way back.

I remember drawing a line on a sheet of paper, writing the words "live life forward." I remember committing to learn from the mistakes I had made and committing to be the kind of person I would be proud of, and that my children would admire.

(Continued)

Before he was a presidential candidate, the former Massachusetts governor Mitt Romney was a lay leader in the Mormon Church near Boston. Here's what he was reported to have told a 19-year-old college student who came to his home: "As human beings, our work isn't measured by taking the sum of our good deeds and the sum of our bad deeds and seeing how things even out. The only thing you need to think about is: Are you trying to improve, are you trying to do better?"[3]

Along with my commitment to "doing better," the Stewardship lessons I was reminded of were: (1) that the truth, no matter how painful and difficult, is always, 100 percent of the time, less painful and less potentially destructive than a secret . . . or a lie; and (2) that worrying about how others will react or what others will think is the surest way to make a bad decision.

Abraham Lincoln, responding to criticism from Congress, is reported to have said in 1862, "I do the very best I know how—the very best I can; and I mean to keep doing so until the end. If the end brings me out all right, what is said against me won't amount to anything. If the end brings me out wrong, 10 angels swearing I was right will make no difference."[4]

That quote, incidentally, was reportedly given by an employee in the basement of the Federal Reserve Bank's headquarters at the height of the financial crisis to none other than Federal Reserve chairman Ben Bernanke.

Stewardship lessons, it seems, come in all shapes and sizes.

Chapter 2

Finance Run Amok

Selfishness Trumps Stewardship

Many of the organizations that failed amidst the market troubles . . . were either muddled about what their missions were or somehow lost their way.

—Al Watts, *Navigating Integrity*

L ate in September 2008, a few days after the bankruptcy filing of Lehman Brothers Holdings, Bruce Bent Sr.'s Reserve Primary Fund broke the buck and suspended redemptions, which effectively froze the cash holdings of hundreds of thousands of individual fund shareholders. Bent's fund was a $62 billion money market fund, a popular savings vehicle that had been viewed as one of the safest, most conservative investments on the planet. Now it was creating life-altering anxiety over whether its clients would ever see their money. And if they did get their money, how much would they get and when would they get it?

Imagine my interest level a few days later when I learned that Bent had approached my parent company, Royal Bank of Canada, with a plan.

Bent's proposal (as I understood it) was to transfer assets out of his existing funds to new, almost identical funds, advised by a newly created investment advisor. This new investment advisor would be jointly owned, Bent proposed, by himself and RBC. The creation of this new controlling vehicle would demote his existing investment advisory entity and the existing funds to mere shell entities that would remain targets of investor litigation and regulatory penalties.

In essence, Bent proposed to appropriate the brand attributes—safety, stability, and security—of Canada's largest and most respected financial institution. As I understood it, he wanted to transform his ownership of a damaged business into partial ownership of a more viable one. In the process, this could deprive his clients of one of the avenues of recourse still potentially available to them—suing Reserve Management, which was Bent's investment advisory firm, and the funds they managed for the lost value of their investments.

Interestingly, Bent didn't propose to include his other business—which owned a patented process that enabled brokerage firms to deposit cash on behalf of their clients into banks, and to get the benefit of FDIC insurance on those deposits. That venture wasn't affected by the Lehman bankruptcy. If anything, it had probably increased in value as investors fled to safety. Bent still wanted to own that outright.

I called Bent on behalf of RBC and told him that we would explore a proposal like his under one condition and one condition only: if we used the profits of any newly created investment entity to make investors in the Reserve Primary Fund whole.

"That's crazy," he told me. "Why would I do that?"

It occurred to me that Bruce Bent Sr.'s attitude was an all-too-prevalent example of the lack of client focus that has gotten us into the crisis.

It didn't take long after that for our conversation to end. As I put down the phone, it occurred to me that Bent's attitude was an all-too-prevalent example of the lack of client focus that had gotten us into the crisis we were in at the time, and was creating panic and confusion for millions of individual and institutional investors.

I channeled my disappointment into a private memo. I didn't distribute it then. But I set out excerpts here:

> I don't consider Bent immoral for holding Lehman Brothers commercial paper, but his proposal to RBC contained what I consider to be too little concern for the well-being of clients who are suffering . . . and that, in my opinion, violates the very premise of Stewardship on which the asset management business is built.
>
> Reserve Primary Fund's clients still don't have access to their cash. They don't know when they will or if they ever will. Every day our firm hears about the hardships this has caused for Reserve shareholders. The fund's board of trustees has retreated behind a wall of secrecy and silence. The SEC at this point is not involved.
>
> I have a suggestion for Bruce Bent: Do everything you can to make your clients whole. At least that way you'll have a chance to emerge from this disaster with your reputation intact.

Arch Villains

Innumerable causes have been cited by innumerable authors, commentators, regulators, and politicians for the financial crisis of 2008–2009. I review many of these causes in this book. I also tell you that I think the key cause of the crisis was a lack of Stewardship values in our society and our financial institutions. Besides Bruce Bent Sr.'s Reserve Primary Fund, I also look at the public record on Goldman Sachs, which, rightly or wrongly, in an industry where perception is reality, became the Wall Street firm most pilloried for its behavior during the crisis.

Let's start with the litany of causes of the crisis. A financial crisis inquiry commission was empaneled by Congress to develop an official explanation, only itself to come up with competing and contradictory explanations. The commission's report identified "lax regulators, reckless bankers, demonic derivatives, heedless borrowers, cynical hedge funds and desultory rating agencies, along with a 'breakdown in ethics' and way too much debt," and one dissenting opinion cited 10 other causes, in particular the credit and housing bubbles.[1]

Jeremy Grantham, one of the most prescient and entertaining commentators on the causes of the crash, blamed "the arch villains,"[2] former Federal Reserve chairman Alan Greenspan and current Federal Reserve chairman Ben Bernanke, in an article he titled, "Night of the Living Fed." In his opinion, their decades-long policy of easy money created a bubble in residential housing and other assets. Grantham joked that just about the only thing he didn't blame the Fed for was climate change, and concluded that they were probably responsible for that as well.[3]

"The crash has been blamed on cheap money, Asian savings and greedy bankers," *The Economist* magazine wrote. "For many people, deregulation is the prime suspect."[4]

A more extreme point of view is expressed in *Thieves' Paradise*, a *New York Times* review of *Griftopia*, by Matt Taibbi (the *Rolling Stone* reporter who coined the phrase *vampire squid* to describe the business practices of Goldman Sachs):

> The nation suffered the equivalent of a hostile takeover of key areas of its commercial life by investment banking houses, while regulators and members of Congress abdicated their responsibilities either because they were influenced by campaign cash or because they believed the fairy tale that unsupervised markets always work best.[5]

A Means to Greater Ends

To this cacophony of primal causes and contributing factors, I would like to add one more. I believe it is a more important and fundamental cause than all the others combined. It is the failure on the part of leaders of some of our largest financial institutions to remain true to the Stewardship mission that defines the financial services industry. It is what Al Watts calls "mission and values drift," in his book *Navigating Integrity*.[6]

Financial institutions are, or ought to be, a means to greater ends. They exist to facilitate and foster economic growth. They act as intermediaries, as go-betweens: They play primarily an agency role, matching up people and organizations that have capital with people and organizations that need capital—frequently putting up their own capital to enhance their agency capabilities. In the case of banks, they match depositors' capital with entities that need capital, including corporations, governments, public agencies, and nonprofit organizations. In the case of money management firms, they match investors' capital with these capital-hungry entities. When true to their mission and purpose, financial institutions execute their agency responsibilities in such a way that everyone wins so that everyone is better off. To do this well, they must be client-focused. Their primary mission must be to serve the needs of their clients, namely depositors, investors, and all the entities using that capital.

In the years leading up to the financial crisis of 2008–2009, financial services firms stopped thinking of themselves as intermediaries whose role was to serve simply as a means to greater ends. They started thinking of themselves as ends unto themselves.

> *Financial institutions . . . play primarily an agency role, matching up people and organizations that have capital with people and organizations that need capital.*

"The proper end of Wall Street is to oil the nation's business," writes Roger Lowenstein in *The End of Wall Street*. "[I]t became, in the bubble era, a goal in itself, a machine wired to inhuman perfection."[7]

Proof points of this include the fact that the share of gross domestic product (GDP) produced by the financial sector more than doubled from 3 percent in 1965 to 7.5 percent in 2010, prompting Jeremy Grantham to observe that "our economy has a painfully overdeveloped financial sector."[8]

The financial sector also experienced a major increase in profitability. Return on equity became a bigger part of many countries' economies, as measured by the amount of debt it issued compared to those countries' entire GDPs. In the United States, for example, financial services debt rose from 34 percent of GDP in 1983 to 120 percent of GDP by 2009.[9]

What drove this growth in the relative importance of financial firms and their simultaneous ability to generate historically outsized returns? Those returns were possible because financial institutions, particularly the larger ones, stopped acting merely as agents on behalf of their clients and started increasingly acting as principals on behalf of themselves. Using more and more leverage, they loaded up their balance sheets with riskier and less liquid assets, supported by less and less capital, pursuing increasingly explicit mandates to make money for their own accounts, creating a culture and set of values different from those of a firm dedicated to helping solve customer problems, facilitate customer orders, or meet customer needs.

As the *Financial Times* put it in a 2011 series titled *Future of Banking,* "With hindsight, it is clear the structure of the [banking] sector in the years before 2007 was an accident waiting to happen. Institutions had grown distorted in the pursuit of bumper profits."[10]

"The failures of . . . Wall Street were failures of individuals to remember that they needed to act, above all, from a sense of agency responsibility," writes Stephen Young in *Moral Capitalism.* "[P]ersonal consciousness of being in an agency relationship vis-à-vis others bears directly on how we will use our power; if we are morally alive and are aware of our status as an agent . . . we will tend not to abuse our position."[11]

This concept of *agency*—which has embedded in it the concept of serving others—is the link between Stewardship principles and moral behavior. It is the corporate equivalent, if you will, of empathy. As Young points out, a moral sense requires sensitivity to "the use of power when others come into view."[12]

"Moral responsibility is a form of Stewardship, of agency, of fiduciary undertaking. . . . It is a vision of mutuality, of service, of both self and others," says Young.[13]

Backlash against Goldman

On April 27, 2010, I was at the U.S. Capitol in a meeting with members of Congress about financial regulatory reform. That day, Goldman Sachs executives were called in to testify before the Senate Permanent Subcommittee on Investigations, chaired by Senator Carl Levin (D-MI). Eleven days earlier, the SEC had charged Goldman with fraud in structuring and marketing collateralized debt obligations tied to subprime mortgages, in particular a transaction known as ABACUS 2007-AC1.

The Goldman hearings were the high-water mark of public outrage. The spark had been the cataclysmic meltdown of financial institutions that began in March 2008 with the collapse of Bear Stearns. It culminated in the spectacle of many of the largest and most recognizable financial institutions in the world writing off billions of dollars of shareholder equity, failing outright, being forced into government takeovers or succumbing to deathbed mergers. Most of these mergers occurred during September 2008, which was the single most turbulent month in the financial services industry since the Great Depression. (See Figure 2.1.)

> *The Goldman hearings were instructive precisely because they illuminated behaviors that took place in the gray zone just this side of outright criminality.*

The subject of the hearings was a small subset of internal e-mails Goldman had produced in response to subpoenas from Levin's committee. The atmosphere was chaotic. Photographers jammed the hallway outside the hearing room, adding to the drama. Protestors in prison uniforms held up placards reading "Shame" and "Stop Looting America."

The normally staid *Economist* was inspired to dub the proceeding "Sachs and the Shitty," referring to a particular line of questioning from Chairman Levin about an e-mail that used the phrase "one shitty deal":

> How about the fact that you sold hundreds of millions of that deal [a CDO named Timberwolf Ltd.] after your people knew it was one shitty deal?[14]

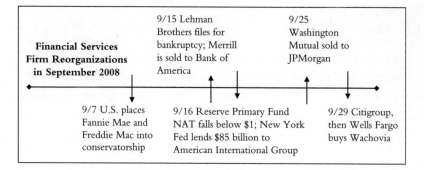

Figure 2.1   September 2008: The Worst Month Since the Great Depression
Source: "The Financial Crisis: A Timeline of Events and Policy Actions," Federal Reserve of St. Louis.

The Goldman hearings were the general public's equivalent of my conversation with Bruce Bent; for many observers, they exposed a failure of Stewardship values and an abdication of Stewardship responsibilities at the core of our financial system.

William D. Cohan's book, *Money and Power: How Goldman Sachs Came to Rule the World,* captures the backlash occasioned by the Goldman hearings and the SEC's charges through a series of interviews with industry observers.

For example, Cohan quotes John C. Coffee, professor of law at Columbia University:

> The SEC's complaint against Goldman raises serious issues about the level of integrity in our capital markets. The idea that an investment banking firm could allow one side in a transaction to design the transaction's terms to favor it over other, less preferred clients of the investment bank (and without disclosure of this influence) disturbs many Americans. . . . Such conduct is not only unfair, it has an adverse impact on investor trust and confidence and thus on the health and efficiency of our capital markets. . . . Once, "placing the customer first" was the clearly understood norm for investment banks, as they knew they could only sell securities to clients who placed their trust and confidence in them. . . . But, with the rise of derivatives and esoteric financial engineering, some firms may have strayed from their former business model.[15]

Michael Greenberger, professor at the University of Maryland School of Law and a former director of trading and markets at the Commodity Futures Trading Commission summed it up this way:

> [T]his idea that "Look, we have loyalties to no one but ourselves. We can be advising both sides of the bet that the bet is good and that's perfectly within the mainstream of the way we do business."[16]

And Sylvain R. Raynes, a former Goldman employee said:

> The simultaneous selling of securities to customers and shorting them because they believed they were going to default is the most cynical use of credit information I have ever seen. When

you buy protection against an event you have a hand in causing, you are buying fire insurance on someone else's house and
then committing arson.[17]

Those who were looking for criminal behavior in the testimony
of Goldman executives were disappointed. But they missed the point.
The Goldman hearings were instructive precisely because they illumi-
nated behaviors that took place in the gray zone, short of criminality.

"The hearing produced no smoking gun, but there was much that
looked bad for Goldman," wrote *The Economist.* "Even its staunchest
supporters would accept that its interests appear murky to outsiders."[18]

Stated Chairman Levin:

> Surely, there's no law, ethical guideline, or moral injunction
> against profit. But Goldman Sachs—it didn't just make money,
> it profited by taking advantage of its clients' reasonable
> expectation[s] that it would not sell products that it did not want
> to succeed and that there was no conflict of economic interest
> between the firm and the customers it had pledged to serve. . . .
> [I]nstead of doing well when its clients did well, Goldman Sachs
> did well when its clients lost money. [Goldman's] conduct brings
> into question the whole function of Wall Street, which tradi-
> tionally has been seen as an engine of growth, betting on
> America's successes, and not its failures.[19]

"It is very hard to find the line between delusion, venality, and outright
corruption," write Bethany McLean and Joe Nocera in *All the Devils Are
Here.* "Much of what took place during the crisis was immoral, unjust,
craven, delusional behavior—but it wasn't criminal."[20]

On July 15, 2010, three months after the Levin hearings, Goldman
Sachs agreed to pay $550 million, and agreed to "reform its business
practices to settle SEC charges that Goldman misled investors in a
subprime mortgage product just as the U.S. housing market was starting
to collapse." Lorin L. Reisner, deputy director of the SEC's Division of
Enforcement, was quoted in an SEC news release stating, "The
unmistakable message of this lawsuit and today's settlement is that half-
truths and deception cannot be tolerated and that the integrity of the
securities markets depends on all market participants acting with

uncompromising adherence to the requirements of truthfulness and honesty."[21]

In the aftermath of the Levin hearings and its settlement with the SEC, Goldman asked former New York Federal Reserve Bank president Gerald Corrigan to conduct an internal soup-to-nuts review of its internal business practices and revised and republished its core principles. The good news is those principles reaffirmed the primacy of service to clients.

> Our clients' interests always come first. Our experience shows that if we serve our clients well, our own success will follow.[22]

The troubling news is—those were exactly the same words in the version of Goldman's core principles that former CEO John Whitehead had written years earlier, and that supposedly served as the firm's true north while the ABACUS deal was being marketed.

As for Bruce Bent Sr. and his son, Bruce Bent II, they were both eventually charged with fraud by the SEC for failing to provide "material facts" prior to suspending redemptions in the Reserve Primary Fund and for engaging "in a systematic campaign to deceive the investing public."[23]

According to the SEC, "[T]hey placed their own financial and reputational interests ahead of the Fund and its shareholders."[24]

Those allegations concisely describe the kind of Stewardship failure this book is all about.

■ ■ ■

Interlude
Occupying Wall Street
Too Rich and Too Poor

A leaderless people powered movement for democracy that
began in America on September 17 with an encampment in
the financial district of New York City. Inspired by the
Egyptian Tahrir Square uprising and the Spanish acampadas,
we vow to end the monied corruption of our democracy.

SOURCE: www.occupywallstreet.org.

The protest movement that started in Zuccotti Park in
Lower Manhattan in the fall of 2011 and sprouted offshoots
in Washington, D.C., Los Angeles, San Francisco, Chicago,
Seattle, even Minneapolis, may be hard for many to take seriously. These full-time protests are a leaderless, diffuse, anarchistic
series of made-for-media gatherings. They have no coherent
message and no understanding of the role of financial institutions
in the economy.

One participant wanted Andrew Jackson's picture removed
from the $20 bill because of his treatment of Native Americans.
Another, from Vermont, told a reporter he wanted "to get rid of
the combustion engine."[25]

But the fact that protesters were still parading around with
signs saying "Make Banks Pay" two and a half years after the U.S.
Senate's "Sachs and the Shitty" hearings on Goldman Sachs is no
laughing matter at all. Nor was an interview with Roseanne Barr,
the comedian, in which she told a newscaster she is "in favor of
the return of the guillotine."[26]

If Occupy Wall Street has any lasting impact, it may have less
to do with its slam Wall Street theatrics and more to do with its
roots in another of the sustainability crises we are eventually
going to face. That crisis, which is also a result of our aban-
donment of Stewardship values and responsibilities, is growing
inequality in the distribution of income and wealth. (See Chapter 8
for a discussion of other sustainability issues.)

(Continued)

"What's the message [of the protestors]?" asked Andrew Ross Sorkin in the *New York Times*. "At times it can be hard to discern, but, at least to me, the message was clear: The demonstrators are seeking accountability . . . for the growing economic inequality gap."[27]

"The one thing we all have in common," wrote a contributor to Occupy Wall Street's website, "is that We Are The 99 percent that will no longer tolerate the greed and corruption of the 1 percent."[28]

Three weeks after the protests began, the International Monetary Fund (IMF) published a report showing income inequality can actually work against long-term economic growth. The study, by authors Andrew Berg and Jonathan Ostry writing in the Fund's *Finance & Development* magazine, analyzed six variables across world economies from 1950 to 2006 and found income distribution more highly correlated with sustainable economic growth than any other factor, including trade openness. The study found that "a 10 percentile decrease in inequality . . . increases the expected length of a growth spell by 50 percent."[29] The IMF study is significant because it confirms that income has become less evenly distributed since the late 1970s, a period Nobel laureate Paul Krugman has labeled the "Great Divergence."

By 2010, the top 20 percent of Americans earned about half of the nation's income, with the top 1 percent earning half of that. The ratio of the average earnings of the top 20 percent to the 15 percent of Americans living in poverty was 14.5 to 1—compared to a historic low of 7.69 to 1 in 1968.

According to the *Huffington Post,* income inequality in the United States "more closely compares to the income distributions of Russia and Iran than many other developed economies."[30] And money-manager-turned-social-commentator Jeremy Grantham observes that "personal income progress [has been] very modest."[31]

"[T]he U.S. continues its odd and long history of flowing all economic gains to corporations and the very rich and basically none to the average hour worked. . . . [O]ur income distribution . . . has become steadily steeper, to the point where we *have become one of the least egalitarian developed societies.*"[32]

Income inequality is anathema not only to sustained economic growth, but to the proper functioning of a democratic political system, both of which depend on the reasonable sharing of benefits.

If we don't address growing inequality, Occupy Wall Street's tech-enabled occupation of public spaces is going to look quaint and harmless compared to the kind of protests we might be faced with down the road. We don't need to go to Tahrir Square in Egypt to see what those might look like. We need only remember the Watts riots, in Los Angeles, in 1965.

Further away in time, perhaps. But a lot closer to home.

Chapter 3

Stewardship Defined

Feeding Your Flock First

Stewardship is the choice for service.
—Peter Block, *Stewardship: Choosing Service Over Self-Interest*

T he word *Stewardship* means something different to almost everyone who uses it. As a practical matter, today the term is most frequently and loosely used to provide a justification for annual fundraising appeals. Those who invoke it often point to its Judeo-Christian origins.

- "The earth is the Lord's, and everything in it, the world, and all who live in it." (Psalm 24:1)
- "To the Lord your God belong the heavens, even the highest heavens, the earth and everything in it." (Deuteronomy 10:14)
- "Everything under heaven belongs to me." (Job 41:11)

And in other biblical verses, there are more than a few admonitions to those who fail to live up to a Stewardship standard, as in

Ezekiel 34:2: "Woe to you shepherds of Israel who only take care of yourselves! Should not shepherds take care of the flock?"[1]

Yet *Stewardship* also has a very secular definition. "Stewardship is to hold something in trust for another," writes author Peter Block. "Historically, Stewardship was a means to protect a kingdom while those rightfully in charge were away."[2] The Merriam-Webster dictionary defines *Stewardship* as "the careful and responsible management of something entrusted to one's care."[3]

All of these definitions capture a part of, but ultimately fall short of, the central quality that makes Stewardship a core principle robust enough to power and undergird our financial system. As Al Watts writes in *Navigating Integrity*:

> We commonly think of stewardship as a caretaking role for resources or affairs entrusted to us . . . However, if we have the "whole picture" in mind, accountability requires adopting a broader perspective on our stewardship role.[4]

Stewardship as a foundational principle has to do with the proposition that one's true purpose—and that the ultimate purpose of organizations and of our communities—is to serve others.

"Stewardship," writes Peter Block, "is the choice for service."[5]

Here we are, returned to the power of Bobby Piper's mission statement for Piper Jaffray & Hopwood: "We . . . believe that serving our clients is our basic purpose. We believe service is the chief contributor to our growth and profitability."

Mission Impossible

An essential prerequisite to the ability to serve others is the ability to subordinate self-interest. Failing that, you must at least be able to set self-interest alongside and balance your interests with the needs of others. "[S]ervice is a moral activity, subordinating self to what is beyond the self," writes Stephen Young, global executive director of the *Caux Round Table*. Expecting financial services executives and their firms to abide by a purely other-oriented virtue alone is probably nothing short of a mission impossible. As Young puts it, "When virtue speaks to us, its voice may be too soft for us to hear." But, "where virtue is supported by claims of interest, our resolve grows stronger to achieve what both virtue and interest jointly propose." Young describes what he calls "the zone of overlap" between virtue and self-interest. "The more we take into account the needs of others when seeking to meet our own needs, the larger the overlap between our self-interest and virtue."[6]

Young also appropriates from Thomas Reid, the phrase "self-interest considered upon the whole."[7] Reid was a Scotsman who succeeded Adam Smith to chair of moral philosophy at the University of Glasgow in 1776.

"Self-interest considered upon the whole" is the best phrase I have found to describe a real world formulation for the kind of Stewardship principle that should undergird and power the financial services industry. It echoes the admonition I received from Larry Summers, director of the White House National Economic Council for President Barack Obama, in the midst of congressional debate about financial regulatory reform: "You people," he said, speaking to a group of financial services executives, "have got to demonstrate that you are willing and able to operate your businesses with one eye on what's good for the country."

In this context, Stewardship means accepting accountability for the impact of one's own actions, the impact of the organization one is leading, and the impact of the industry one belongs to, on the larger community.

> *"You people have got to demonstrate that you are willing and able to operate your businesses with one eye on what's good for the country."*
>
> —Larry Summers

There are many parallels between the concept of Stewardship and that of *servant leadership*, a term created by the late Robert K. Greenleaf in a 1970 essay titled *The Servant as Leader*. Greenleaf, who was born in Terre Haute, Indiana, spent most of his career, some 40 years, at AT&T. Greenleaf later served as a consultant to a number of institutions, including Ohio University, MIT, the Ford Foundation, the Richard King Mellon Foundation, the Mead Corporation, the American Foundation for Management Research, and the Lilly Endowment. In 1964, Greenleaf founded the Center for Applied Ethics, now the Robert K. Greenleaf Center, headquartered in Indiana.

Greenleaf distilled learning from his consulting career in a series of essays and books on the theme of the servant as leader, with the objective of stimulating thought and action for building a better, more caring society.[8]

Inherent in Greenleaf's construct of servant leadership is the leader's belief that whatever they are doing, they are doing it in the service of, and for the sake of, others.

"Servant leadership, like stewardship, assumes first and foremost a commitment to serving the needs of others," writes Larry Spears, former director of the Greenleaf Center. "True leadership emerges from those whose primary motivation is a desire to help others."[9]

I know that whenever I have assumed a new leadership role, I have been inspired by the sense of having been called. I have felt a recognition that my responsibility is to lead, manage, and operate the organization as effectively as I can for the benefit of its constituents. In 2005, when I became CEO of RBC Wealth Management-U.S., that meant individual investor clients, employees, and shareholders. In 2009, when I became chairman-elect of the Securities Industry and Financial Markets Association (SIFMA), that meant securities dealers and asset management member firms. In all cases, I felt it was my responsibility to lead, manage, and operate the organization for the benefit of a broader constituency— consistent with servant leadership. As author Larry Spears writes in his collection of essays on Greenleaf's philosophy:

> Greenleaf's view of all institutions was one in which CEOs, staffs, directors, and trustees all played significant roles in holding their institutions in trust for the greater good of society.[10]

Stewardship is also closely aligned with the concept of fiduciary duty, which is another term that gets bandied about without a clear or consistent understanding of what it exactly means. As is the case with Stewardship, a fiduciary mindset requires a sense of obligation to others. Writes Stephen Young in his book *Moral Capitalism*, "Fiduciary obligations flow from a principle within the moral sense that sensitizes us to the use of power when others come into view."[11] Young goes on to suggest that a sense of moral responsibility is a common characteristic of "stewardship, of agency, of fiduciary undertaking," as is "a vision of mutuality, of service, of both self and others."[12]

Purposefulness

The chief attribute of Stewardship, of servant leadership, and of fiduciary obligation, is a strong and abiding sense of purpose. It is a capacity—call it purposefulness—to remain focused on and true to that sense of purpose. Or, to put it a little differently, "the ability to see enough choices of aims, to choose the right aim and to pursue that aim responsibly over a long period of time."[13]

In *Navigating Integrity*, Al Watts points out the pressures leaders in today's world are forced to deal with. They are required to keep up with a faster and faster pace of change, but also they are expected to make an increasing number of decisions on a daily basis as a result of the way technology has shortened the timeline for almost every business process. In this environment, writes Watts, "Competitive and market pressures, a drive for growth, investor expectations or distractions veiled as opportunities make it difficult to stay 'on mission' unless we are very clear about our purpose and values."[14] That's true of many industries, but none more so than the financial services industry, where markets can and do change literally overnight; where three standard-deviation events occur with disruptive regularity; and where time to market and the shelf life of new ideas is often measured in days or weeks rather than years. In an environment like that, "purpose is the difference between good and great," writes Watts, quoting Nikos Mourkogiannis, author of *Purpose*.

Watts uses the image of a lead keel on a sailboat as a perfect analogy for a characteristic like purposefulness, "keeping us generally headed in the right direction and assuring that we can always recover, even in turbulent seas."[15]

Other attributes of Stewardship include:

Humility

As Peter Block puts it in his book *Stewardship*, "There is pride in leadership, it evokes images of direction. There is humility in stewardship, it evokes images of service."[16]

Doug Lennick and Fred Kiel tell us in *Moral Intelligence 2.0* that "leaders at the helm of the perennially great companies all share a common trait—humility."[17]

Paul Purcell, chairman, president and CEO of Robert W. Baird & Company, cites the tenure of E. Stanley O'Neal as CEO of Merrill Lynch from 2002 to 2007 as a case in which arrogance and lack of humility led to "one of worst examples of stewardship failures in my lifetime."[18]

O'Neal—who told Howard University students in a 2004 convocation speech, "This is a world of 'haves' and 'have nots,' and if you want to make a difference, it helps to be a 'have' "[19]—resigned after Merrill's mortgage-backed securities holdings led to the largest loss in the firm's history. A payout estimated at $159 million cushioned the blow.

"Merrill Lynch was one of the greatest franchises in the world," Purcell told me in an interview. "It was virtually bullet-proof. But O'Neal managed to stuff the balance sheet full of mortgages and literally blew the place up—all because he wanted to outcompete Goldman Sachs and J.P. Morgan!"[20]

Accountability

There is a component of Stewardship that is all about the willingness "to be deeply accountable for the outcomes of an institution."[21] In other words . . . "the buck stops here" kind of ethic. In fact, as Stephen Young suggests, a requirement of effective Stewardship may be "that we think of ourselves as holding an office."[22]

> We always have an office to perform in the markets of capitalism. In that office—be it buyer or seller, worker or investor—we need to be honest and reliable and to assert our self-interest with a view toward the whole.[23]

Young invokes the concept of community and suggests that we think of our actions in terms of their impact on our neighbors. He goes on to ask, "Who then . . . is my neighbor? The answer seems to be— persons who are so closely and directly affected by my act that I ought reasonably to have them in contemplation as being so affected when I am directing my mind to the acts or omissions which are called in question."[24]

Accountability, as stated earlier, means being aware of and assuming responsibility for the effect our actions have on others, with *others* defined as broadly as possible.

Foresight

Effective Stewardship requires us to do two things, both of which are captured beautifully by the Japanese samurai-turned-Zen-philosopher Miyamoto Musashi:

1. "See distant things, as they are close."
2. "[See] close things, as they are distant."[25]

Foresight is the central ethic of leadership, says Robert Greenleaf. It is critical, if we are to effectively manage organizations for the benefit of their constituents, that leaders "see future events . . . before other people see them."[26] This is the second part of Musashi's advice—"see close things, as they are distant." Greenleaf points out that serious ethical compromises are often attributable to yesterday's failure to foresee today and take the right actions yesterday. The result may be ethically bad choices because the leeway within which to initiate action has been narrowed and only bad choices remain.[27]

The first part of Mushahsi's advice, however, has to do with what Native Americans call *seventh-generation thinking*—"the ability to see the distant effect of our decisions and actions today—where 'distance' may be measured in many miles or many generations."[28]

The Great Binding Law of the Iroquois Nation admonishes us to "look and listen for the welfare of the whole people and have always in view not only the present but the coming generations . . . the unborn of the future Nation."[29]

This concept of looking out for the consequences of today's actions (or inactions) on future generations is critical to the concept of Stewardship.

Integrity

"If you do not have integrity, no one will trust you, nor should they," says John C. Bogle.[30]

Trust is central to all human interaction. And it is particularly critical to the functioning of financial markets. "Markets will not survive without trust. . . . Where cheating and mistrust and broken promises prevail, markets are shrunken and reduced to barter and economic minimalism," writes Stephen Young.[31]

In *Moral Intelligence*, Doug Lennick and Fred Kiel write, "Integrity is the hallmark of the morally intelligent person." And they quote the Chinese proverb, "To starve to death is a small thing, but to lose one's integrity is a great one."[32]

> *Trust is central to all human interaction. And it is particularly critical to the functioning of financial markets.*

"Our system of capitalism is built on trust," writes former Medtronic CEO Bill George in *Authentic Leadership*. "[T]rust that corporate leaders and boards of directors will be good stewards of their resources."[33]

Purposefulness. Humility. Accountability. Foresight. Integrity.

These are not the words that come to mind when we think back on the behaviors of leaders of some of our largest financial institutions during 2008 and 2009. One need only read Charley Ellis's description of which "certain factors" are "important in any great firm" to see how far the Goldman Sachs of Senator Levin's hearing had strayed from its one-time Stewardship values. Ellis wrote about these factors in his book *The Partnership*, written just before the onset of the financial crisis.

> [C]ertain factors are important in every great firm: long-serving and devoted "servant leaders"; meritocracy in compensation and authority; disproportionate devotion to client service; distinctively high professional and ethical standards; a strong culture that always reinforces professional standards of excellence; and

long-term values, policies, concepts and behavior consistently trumping near-term "opportunities."[34]

The obvious question is whether it was possible for a Stewardship ethic to prevail among our leading financial institutions in the years leading up to and during the financial crisis. Another critical question is: Would things have turned out differently if a Stewardship ethic had prevailed? In fact, that's exactly what happened in the Canadian banking system. Let's turn now to see what that looked like, and why and how the Canadian experience was so different from that in the United States and other developed societies.

■ ■ ■

Interlude
Greed, Glorious Greed

Following disclosures that a "rogue trader" generated losses of $2.3 billion at the global bank UBS and just before the resignation of their CEO, Oswald Grübel, the *New York Times*'s James B. Stewart criticized the bank's Stewardship failures in an article titled, "At UBS, It's the Culture That's Rogue."[35]

"The financial crisis and its aftermath have proved daunting for most of the world's banks, but in many ways UBS's behavior stands out," wrote the *Times*. The article referred to:

- A $160 million fine UBS agreed to pay in connection with its admission "that its employees had conspired to rig bids in the municipal bond derivatives market."

- UBS's "prominent role in recent notorious tax evasion cases" involving secret bank accounts for some "17,000 wealthy Americans" that allowed them to evade income taxes. UBS was threatened with criminal prosecution and "agreed to pay a $781 million fine and divulge the names of account holders, effectively ending the historic[al] tradition of Swiss bank secrecy and prompting a rush of United States taxpayers to confess to the IRS."

- UBS's "headlong rush into the ill-fated mortgage-backed securities market before it collapsed in 2008," was described as "one of the worst blunders in banking history." As a result of which "UBS absorbed a staggering $38 billion in losses and had to be bailed out by the Swiss government."

The *Times* saved its most acerbic language, however, for UBS's response to the freezing up of the auction-rate securities market in 2008, something *New York Times* reporter Stewart is personally familiar with. Auction-rate securities, or ARS, are long-term debt or preferred stock issued either by state and local governmental units and not-for-profit agencies (like student loan finance agencies) and closed-end mutual funds. ARS were a source of low-rate financing. The securities carried a low rate because the rate was set for relatively short periods, usually 7 to 30 days, at the end of which investors could tell their broker-dealers they wanted out of their holdings. Market makers, like UBS, would use their best efforts to auction ARS to new investors, setting the interest rate at a level that cleared the market.

In early 2008, at the beginning of the financial crisis, the market for ARS froze up, almost overnight, stranding investors with long-term bonds and preferred stock. Investors had no way to convert their auction-rate securities to cash.

What happened then is regulators stepped in and charged UBS with misconduct, writes the *New York Times*.

> In August 2008, UBS settled charges brought by Andrew Cuomo, then the New York attorney general, that it misled customers when it sold them what it described as nearly risk-free auction-rate securities even as its executives knew the market was collapsing. After the market froze and investors were unable to sell the securities, regulators sued, and UBS agreed to repay $19.4 billion and pay a $150 million fine.[36]

UBS was far from the only bank that sold ARS, nor was it the only bank that had to reimburse clients.

> . . . what distinguished the UBS case was the allegation that top officials knew the market was collapsing and nonetheless moved to dump its inventory onto unsuspecting clients. E-mails from David Shulman, then global head of municipal securities for UBS, described the securities as an "albatross" and told the bank to "mobilize the troops," adding "the pressure is on to move inventory." Mr. Shulman even sold securities from his own personal account just before the market collapsed, later settling insider trading charges and agreeing to pay $2.75 million. "While thousands of UBS customers received no warning about the auction-rate securities market's serious distress, David Shulman—one of the company's top executives—used insider information to take the money and run," said Mr. Cuomo.[37]

(*Continued*)

Contrast UBS's auction-rate securities behavior with that of Robert W. Baird & Co., a regional investment banking, brokerage, and asset management firm based in Milwaukee, Wisconsin. Baird, which is employee-owned, is run by chairman, president, and CEO Paul Purcell, who's known in the industry for speaking his mind.

"When the auction-rate securities market froze up," Purcell told me, "we went to our clients, on day one, and said to them: 'We will make you whole. We can't do it right now, because we don't have the capital to buy back your holdings. But if you give us time, and let us work through this, we promise you, we won't lose money and you will get the money you invested back."

Baird made offers to clients facing liquidity hardships to lend them money, secured by their ARS holdings, at interest rates that matched what the ARS were paying. In other words, at a zero percent net interest cost.

"It worked. Eventually we bought back $160 million in ARS holdings from our clients. We didn't get sued and none of our investors lost money. That's something I'm very proud of," Purcell said.

When I asked Purcell whether the ARS crisis belied a larger Stewardship failure in the financial services industry, he jumped all over the question.

"Absolutely. There's no question our industry has lost its way. Not just the big firms. But the bigger firms get, the more focused they seem to become on pushing proprietary products, on finding ways to make money on all sides of a transaction—structuring, selling, hedging, trading—to the detriment of their clients.

"It's greed, glorious greed," Purcell said.[38]

Chapter 4

World's Safest Banking System

Canada, the New Switzerland

Bank executives really do use the word "we" in Canada a lot more than they do in the United States.

— Chris Crosby, former RBC chief strategy officer

In January 2011, I attended the annual meeting of the shareholders of Royal Bank of Canada in Toronto. It took place at the cavernous Metro Toronto Convention Centre, a short walk from the Bank's headquarters down Front Street, along the northern shore of Lake Ontario. RBC is not only the largest financial institution in Canada, but it's my employer. RBC is the Toronto-based parent company of RBC Wealth Management-U.S., for which I have worked since 2001. RBC Wealth Management-U.S. is based in Minneapolis and was formerly the U.S. brokerage firm Dain Rauscher.

I'm an American who also has a strong personal connection to Canada. I went to Toronto to better understand how my Canadian parent company, RBC, has achieved its remarkable record of financial and managerial Stewardship. Even more impressive is that RBC's record of financial strength and fiscal responsibility occurred during a period when thousands of financial institutions around the world went bankrupt or were on the brink of failure. This enviable record of my parent company played an important part in my being named the first Canadian bank executive to chair a U.S. financial trade group, the U.S. Securities Industry and Financial Markets Association. Of course, it also helped that the division of RBC that I head has its headquarters in the United States and that I am an American.

At the 2011 annual meeting, when many of the world's financial institutions were still reeling, RBC announced record earnings of C$1.84 billion for the first quarter of their 2011 fiscal year; the seventh quarter in a row in which the bank had generated over $1 billion in cash earnings. Also, CEO Gordon Nixon told shareholders that RBC was rock-solid even by more-stringent new standards. With a Tier One capital ratio of 13.2 percent,[1] RBC anticipated that it could earn its way into full compliance with proposed tougher international banking capital requirements, known as Basel III, years ahead of the phased-in implementation schedule required by Basel III—without the need to raise additional capital.

And if that wasn't enough good news for shareholders, Nixon also announced RBC would maintain its $2.00 per share dividend, which had increased steadily and been paid without interruption since 1925, with the exception of being cut twice during the Depression and once during World War II.

The story of how RBC and other Canadian banks not only survived but prospered during the financial crisis is well known to Canadians and a source of considerable pride. "Canadian regulators have been doing victory laps for the last three years," says Robert Wessel, managing partner at Hamilton Capital Partners, a Toronto-based boutique investment firm.[2]

Others have taken notice as well.

Shortly after he was elected president of the United States, Barack Obama traveled to the Ottawa residence of Canadian prime minister Stephen Harper, his first visit to a foreign head of state. While he was there, Obama expressed his admiration for the Canadian banking system. "In the midst of the enormous economic crisis, I think Canada has shown itself to be a pretty good manager of the financial system and the economy in ways that we haven't always been," the president said.[3]

For the fourth year in a row (2008 to 2011), Canadian banks have been ranked the soundest banking systems in the world by the World Economic Forum.[4] Their rank comes in first among more than 130 countries.

In early 2010, the *Financial Times* described the Canadian banking system as "a real-world, real-time example of a banking system in a medium-sized, advanced capitalist economy that worked" and went on to suggest that, "understanding why the Canadian system survived could be a key to making the rest of the [W]est equally robust."[5]

The IMF also gives Canada's banks high praise. Here is what it said in its Financial Stability Assessment on Canada: "Canada's financial system is mature, sophisticated, and well-managed. Financial stability is underpinned by sound macroeconomic policies and strong prudential regulations and supervision. Deposit insurance and arrangements for crisis management and failure resolution are well-designed."[6]

One Canadian bank CEO was told by prospective clients that "Canada has become the new Switzerland." As if to prove that point, in 2011, Mark Carney, the governor of the Bank of Canada, was named the chairman of the Basel, Switzerland-based Financial Stability Board, the international body that includes all major G-20 nations and supranational organizations and, as we will see in the next chapter, monitors and makes recommendations about the global financial system.

> *"[U]nderstanding why the Canadian system survived could be a key to making the rest of the [W]est equally robust."*
>
> —*Financial Times*

Canada was the only G-7 country that did not require a government-funded bank bailout during the financial crisis, as you can see in Figure 4.1. Canadian banks remained profitable throughout 2008 and 2009; no Canadian bank even cut its dividend. In 2009, 140 banks failed in the United States; 157 failed in 2010.[7] The count of failed U.S. financial institutions over the past century is in the thousands. During the same period, three Canadian banks failed: the Home Bank of Canada—representing about 1 percent of the banking system's total assets—collapsed in 1923. Northland Bank and the Canadian Commercial Bank failed in 1985, representing, together,

Total public sector liquidity extension

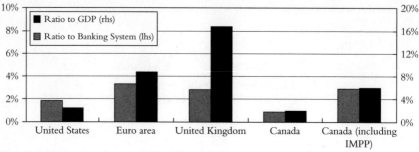

Note: Liquidity extension refers to central banks' liquidity-providing operations, as well as foreign currency swaps with other central banks, but excludes outright securities purchases.

Figure 4.1   Canadian Banks Get Fewer Government Handouts
Sources: Bank of Canada, U.S. Federal Reserve, Bank of England, and European Central Bank. Reprinted with permission of the Bank of Canada. Originally printed in: "Canada and the Economic Crisis: Our Performance and Near-Term Prospects," by John Murray, September 15, 2009, 26, www .bankofcanada.ca/wp-content/uploads/2010/03/presentation_murray150909.pdf.

Cumulative writedowns as a share of shareholders' equity

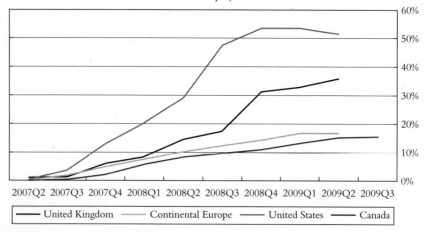

Figure 4.2   Canadian Banks Say No Thanks to Risk
Sources: Bloomberg and banks' financial statements. Reprinted with permission of the Bank of Canada. Originally printed in: "Canada and the Economic Crisis: Our Performance and Near-Term Prospects," by John Murray, September 15, 2009, 26, www.bankofcanada.ca/wp-content/uploads/2010/03/presentation_murray150909.pdf.

roughly 0.75 percent of total banking system assets.[8] Clearly, Canadian banks have a conservative risk appetite (see Figure 4.2).

Over the period from 2005 to 2010, total returns for shareholders in Canadian banks dwarfed those of banks in the United States and the United Kingdom. See Figure 4.3.

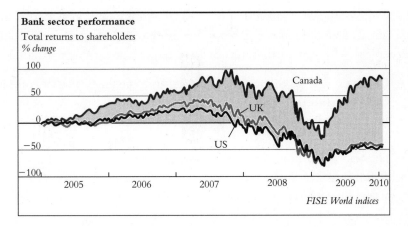

Figure 4.3 What Toronto Can Teach New York and London
SOURCE: *Financial Times*, January 29, 2010.
DATA SOURCE: Thomas Reuters Datastream.

During August 2011, a period of the most extreme volatility in financial stocks since 2008, Canadian banks once again outperformed their global counterparts, declining only 4 percent compared to an average decline of 18 percent for major U.S. banks and an average decline of 30 percent for European banks.[9]

The Canadian banking story demonstrates that it is possible to design a banking system to withstand stresses of the magnitude that brought banks in other developed nations to their knees in 2008 and 2009—even when that system is dominated by financial institutions that are unequivocally too big to fail. Six banks dominate the Canadian economy, accounting for 90 percent of the deposits in the country's banking system.[10] Those banks are Royal Bank of Canada (RBC), Toronto-Dominion Bank (TD), Bank of Nova Scotia (Scotiabank), Bank of Montreal (BMO), Canadian Imperial Bank of Commerce (CIBC), and National Bank of Canada. Most are based in the central business district of Toronto. And five of those six banks are among the top 10 largest companies in Canada, ranked by profit.[11]

Canada's success is hopeful news for all of us.

We need to understand the specific factors that contributed to Canada's record of banking stability and resilience, and understand which of those factors can be exported to banking systems in other countries.

Commentators generally point to the following key factors to explain Canadian banking stability during the 2008 financial crisis and to explain why Canadian banks did not require government bailouts:

- Canada's system of housing finance and the high quality of the Canadian mortgage markets
- A single dominant federal regulator with a principles-based approach
- Higher capital ratios and lower leverage ratios
- A funding structure and a universal banking model that provided access to stable retail deposits

High Quality Mortgage Market

Canada's mortgage market operates on what is called an *originate-to-hold* model rather than an *originate-to-sell,* or securitization, model. That means Canadian banks hold most of the mortgage loans they make to homeowners rather than packaging and selling them to third-party investors.

From 1970 to 2007, Canadian bank mortgage holdings climbed from 10 percent to 69 percent of the market, representing almost exclusively prime mortgages. During the same time period, U.S. depository institutions' market share of U.S. bank mortgage holdings fell to 30 percent from 75 percent.[12]

The benefits of this are that underwriting standards remained far tighter in Canada than in the United States and other countries. For example—mortgage loans in Canada are full-recourse loans. Borrowers' obligation to pay extends beyond the value of their homes. This is not surprising—since, as holders of the loans, the banks retain the full risk of those loans. The result was far fewer subprime mortgages being made and far fewer troubled loans on the balance sheets of Canadian banks. Whereas mortgage arrears of 90 days or more exceeded 3.5 percent in the United States in March 2009, in Canada the rate was less than 0.5 percent.[13]

The downside, if you can call it that, of the Canadian system of housing finance is that borrowers do not have ready access to long-term fixed-rate loans, since there is no way for banks to fund those loans without securitization. And if borrowers choose to prepay, there is the potential of a prepayment penalty. While Canadian mortgages generally have 30-year terms and are amortized over those 30 years, interest rates are usually variable. Rates are set for periods of six months to five years, and adjusted after that. Also, mortgage interest is not deductible against taxes. None of these features seem like much of a disadvantage, since homeownership rates in Canada and the United States are "virtually identical at about 68 percent of all households."[14]

Principles–Based Regulation

A single, politically independent, federal, prudential regulator supervises Canada's federally chartered banks: the Office of the Superintendent of Financial Institutions (OSFI). It supervises banks and insurance firms and operates by declaring and enforcing guiding principles.

While U.S. regulators tend to operate by what is known as a rules-based rather than a principles-based approach, OSFI's focus tends to be on material risk and the quality of risk management controls in the institutions it supervises. As the *Financial Times* observes, "It is about the spirit, rather than the letter, of the law."[15]

Toronto-Dominion CEO Ed Clark puts it a bit differently: "The message in the U.S. is it's your responsibility to meet our rules. In Canada, the responsibility is to run the institution right."[16]

"The relationship between the government and banks is a positive one," Canada's minister of finance, James Flaherty, told *Time* magazine in 2008, at the height of the crisis. "The common goal is a sound financial system."[17]

Capital and Leverage Ratios

OSFI imposes limits on bank leverage, focusing on the ratio of total assets to total capital. That limit is between 20 and 23 times assets to capital, with assets including certain off-balance-sheet activities. The exact ratio is assigned to a bank according to its risk profile.[18] As Figure 4.4 shows, these leverage ratios are lower than those in the

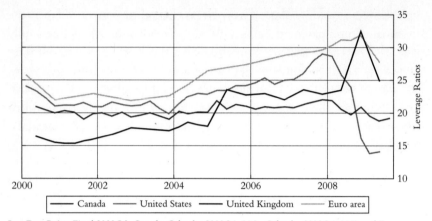

Last Data Point: Fiscal 2009Q2, Canada; Calendar 2009Q1, U.S.; Calendar 2008Q4, U.K. and Europe

Figure 4.4 Canadian Banks Have Less Debt and More Equity
Sources: Bloomberg and banks' financial statements. Reprinted with permission of the Bank of Canada. Originally printed in: "Canada and the Economic Crisis: Our Performance and Near-Term Prospects," by John Murray, September 15, 2009, 26, www.bankofcanada.ca/wp-content/uploads/2010/03/presentation_murray150909.pdf.

United States, the United Kingdom, and the European Union, which before the crisis reached into the high 20s and low 30s.[19] In 2007, the five key investment banks in the United States had leverage ratios of 40.[20] At the end of that year, the combined leverage ratio of Fannie Mae and Freddie Mac was 75.[21]

In addition, OSFI's requirements for the amount of capital Canadian banks need to hold to support their activities has historically been higher than in other countries. Going into the financial crisis, Canadian banks were required to have Tier One capital ratios of 7 percent and total capital ratios of 10 percent. Those are more-stringent requirements than the so-called Basel II international banking requirements of 4 percent and 8 percent, respectively. Just as important, Canadian banks were required to have considerably more of their Tier One capital in the form of common equity, some 75 percent, as compared to the 50 percent required under Basel II.[22] This means that for every $1.00 of risk-weighted assets, Canadian banks were required to have a little more than $.05 in equity, whereas some European banks could have had as little as $.02 in equity.

Funding Structure

Over the past several decades, Canada's regulators have permitted—some would say encouraged—financial institutions to consolidate and, through numerous acquisitions, develop into diversified national institutions that operate as universal banks. Each bank usually operates with three main business lines: retail banking, wholesale banking and capital markets, and wealth management.

Using terms such as *a fortress domestic banking sector* and *mature dominant oligopoly*, Rob Wessel, managing partner at Hamilton Capital Partners, tells us "Canadian regulation sought to create large, domestically powerful banks. They succeeded."[23]

One benefit of this is that Canadian banks have historically been able to attract, and fund themselves, with significant retail banking deposits. One-stop shopping for most financial services creates an important incentive for Canadian consumers to deposit their money with their banks. Retail deposits fund about 65 percent of bank assets, diminishing the need for less sticky wholesale funding.[24] The International Monetary Fund concluded in a 2009 study titled "Why Are Canadian Banks More Resilient?" that a high deposit-to-asset ratio was a key factor explaining Canadian bank resilience.[25] (See Table 4.1.)

Conservative Culture

There is another factor commentators point to in trying to explain the relative outperformance of the Canadian banking system—and that is culture. Observers usually focus on the innate conservatism of Canadians. In her *Financial Times* article, titled "What Toronto can teach New York and London," Chrystia Freeland quotes Matthew Winkler, editor-in-chief of Bloomberg News: "Canadians are like hobbits. They are just not as rapacious as Americans."[26] Freeland also quotes Toronto-Dominion's CEO, Ed Clark, saying, "U.S. bankers see themselves as more important than we do." Her article goes on to say, "In Clark's view, Canadian culture imposes a limit on CEO megalomania: 'Canada is a more egalitarian society; Canadians are less hierarchical. In the U.S., you can tell people to do something. In Canada, you have to ask them to do something—and hope they will do it!' "[27]

Table 4.1   Canadian Banks' Secret of Stability: How Much of Their Assets Are Funded by Core Deposits

Bank	Country	Depository Funding*
Twelve Most Vulnerable		
1 Hypo Real Estate Holding AG	Germany	24.0
2 Northern Rock Plc	United Kingdom	28.7
3 Deutsche Bank AG	Germany	34.1
4 BNP Paribas	France	36.7
5 Citigroup, Inc.	United States	37.8
6 HBOS Plc	United Kingdom	41.0
7 Societe Generale	France	42.0
8 Banca Monte dei Paschi di Siena SpA	Italy	44.1
9 Dexia	Belgium	44.9
10 DnB Nor ASA	Norway	45.4
11 Danske Bank A/S	Denmark	46.3
12 Commerzbank AG	Germany	47.0
Rest of the Sample		
13 JPMorgan Chase & Co.	United States	47.3
14 Barclays Plc	United Kingdom	47.7
15 Bank of America Corporation	United States	47.9
21 National Australia Bank	Australia	51.7
24 Commonwealth Bank of Australia	Australia	53.4
26 HSBC Holdings Plc	United Kingdom	54.9
28 Credit Suisse Group	Switzerland	55.6
30 Capital One Financial Corporation	United States	57.3
32 Lloyds TSB Group Plc	United Kingdom	58.7
33 Royal Bank of Scotland Group Plc (The)	United Kingdom	59.3
44 Wachovia Corporation	United States	62.8
46 UBS AG	Switzerland	64.1
48 Wells Fargo & Company	United States	64.4
51 Royal Bank of Canada (RBC)	*Canada*	*65.1*
52 Banque de Montreal–Bank of Montreal	*Canada*	*65.2*
54 Australia & New Zealand Banking Group	Australia	65.4
57 Toronto-Dominion Bank	*Canada*	*67.9*
60 Canadian Imperial Bank of Commerce	*Canada*	*68.2*
64 Bank of Nova Scotia (The)	*Canada*	*71.4*
68 Westpac Banking Corporation	Australia	74.1
69 Washington Mutual Inc.	United States	74.6

*Depository funding over total assets. *Source:* BankScope and staff calculations.
SOURCE: Lev Ratnovski and Rocco Huang, "Why Are Canadian Banks More Resilient?" IMF Working Paper 09/152, July 2009, Table 4.

"It sounds like a cliché, but it really isn't," says former RBC chief strategy officer Chris Crosby, who left the United States to work in Canada for five years. "Bank executives really do use the word *we* in Canada a lot more than they do in the United States."[28]

> *"Canadians are like hobbits. They are just not as rapacious as Americans."*
> —Matthew Winkler, editor-in-chief of Bloomberg News

I have had considerable personal exposure to Canadian culture. My great-grandfather, U.S. President William Howard Taft, bought vacation property in the early 1900s on the north shore of the St. Lawrence River, in the small resort community of La Malbaie after traveling to Montreal to attend a family wedding. The town is 90 miles or so from Quebec City, the capital of the Canadian province of Quebec. Because of this legacy, I spent the first 20 summers of my life in La Malbaie with my extended family—dozens of aunts, uncles, and cousins shuttling between several houses in what became known as the Taft Compound. Two of the three houses were owned by President Taft's children: the late Helen Manning, one-time dean of Bryn Mawr College; and the late Charles Phelps Taft, one-time mayor of Cincinnati, Ohio. We are a family of Americans who have strong ties to Canada. For the past decade, I have worked for Royal Bank of Canada, heading up businesses in both the United States and in Canada. I am married to a native, bilingual Quebecoise and have two bilingual stepchildren. While I speak French, my stepchildren tell me that I am nowhere near fluent. I have a home in Montreal, the second-largest city in Canada.

In my opinion, there are significant cultural differences between the United States and Canada. But insofar as they played out in the resilience of Canadian banking, I believe these differences go beyond mere conservatism to a more tangible Stewardship ethic in Canada than that which is present today in the United States.

In short, the sense of community that exists at the national level in Canada has somehow become frayed and dissipated in the United States. Community and Stewardship are two sides of the same coin; you can't have one without the other. Communities exist and communities work when their members care about each other. The more strongly community members own a sense of responsibility to each other, the more vital that community becomes.

Unfortunately, in the United States today, "the building blocks of community life—extended families, social clubs, religious organizations, and the like—are in decline."[29] And size itself has worked against community ethics. There is something about community that is intimate and requires personal connections to take root. The larger a demographic group, the more anonymous each member of the community becomes; and the less we feel a connection to and responsibility for the well-being of others in the community.

It may simply be that the relatively small size of Canada—its population of more than 34 million is less than that of the state of California (more than 37 million)—has something to do with an enduring sense of community at the national level. Or it may be the oligopolistic nature of Canada's banking system: Whenever any one of the CEOs of Canada's six largest banks looks outside his window, he sees a client of his bank in one out of every three to five people walking along the street. That might be one reason why they behaved more responsibly than their counterparts in the United States.

> *[T]he sense of community that exists at the national level in Canada has somehow become frayed and dissipated in the United States.*

But for whatever reasons, in the years leading up to and during the financial crisis, the leaders of Canadian banks bucked the trend and were very successful. The CEOs and their management teams and their boards of directors managed their businesses as effective stewards should manage their businesses. They managed their banks the way presidential aide Larry Summers once told the Securities Industry and Financial Markets Association board of directors they should be managed: "with one eye on what's good for [your] country."

■ ■ ■

Interlude
Americans Are from Mars, Canadians Are from Venus

Shortly after making a couple of major acquisitions in the United States, RBC thought cultural differences between Canadian and American employees and customers was a significant business issue. To head off any friction or misunderstandings with the employees of its new American units, RBC commissioned and circulated a PowerPoint presentation. The purpose was to sensitize senior executives to the basic cultural differences between Canadians and Americans. One of these differences, tellingly, is that Canadians do just about everything to avoid mistakes, whereas Americans view making mistakes as a necessary part of being successful.

This analysis of the deep-seated differences between Americans and Canadians was titled *Americans are from Mars, Canadians are from Venus.*[30] The presentation looked at differences in culture, identity, and values that define Canadians and Americans and tied those to differences in geography, climate, and history. They concluded that, "Essentially, America is a masculine culture and Canada is a feminine culture."

For example, while Canadians value a kinder, gentler, civilized society, Americans value personal freedom. While Canadians value pragmatism, Americans value idealism. Canadians value peace, order, the middle, quality of life, tolerance, compassion. The animal that best represents Canadians is the beaver. Americans can best be understood by the eagle.

Canadians and Americans also differ when it comes to their attitudes toward risk.

Canada

- Never change something that works.
- Keeping what you have is preferable to searching for something better.

(Continued)

- Plan ahead for the future.
- Incremental change is best.
- Doing nothing is a perfectly acceptable course of action.
- Never bet more than you can afford to lose.

United States

- Nothing ventured, nothing gained.
- Action is salvation.
- Procrastination is a sin.
- Just do it!
- Go for it.
- The bigger the risk, the bigger the payoff.

Importantly, the study describes Canadian culture as much better suited than American culture to the attributes of Stewardship we have discussed in this chapter. Canadians identify their country as a place. Not just place in terms of physical space, but the "best place in the world." As a result, they value "keeping what they have."

The presentation describes the energy of the country as a "winter energy," in which climate is about survival.

- "In winter in Winnipeg, you can die just by forgetting your house keys."
- "Canadians rely on others for survival."
- "In a cold climate, interdependence is essential. In Canada, risk is the difference between safety and death."

This leads to a sense, for Canadians, that "the collective" is more important than the individual.

It is Canadian attitudes toward time that point most strongly to their capacity for Stewardship.

- "When in doubt, wait and see."
- "Waiting is often the best course of action."

- "We're here to stay so we can afford to wait for what we want."
- "We act for future generations that may come after us."
- "Our time horizon is very long term."
- "We have been around for a long time."
- "We will always be here."

Chapter 5

Making the System Stronger

In Defense of Dodd-Frank and Basel III

Perhaps the biggest casualty of the crisis has been the idea that financial markets are inherently self-correcting and best left to their own devices. After decades of deregulation in most rich countries, finance is entering a new age of reregulation.

—Jonathan Rosenthal, "Chained but Untamed," *The Economist*

The Canadian financial system worked in ways the financial system in the United States and other developed economies did not. The question is this: Will regulatory reform in the United States and around the world move the United States and the global financial systems closer to the Canadian system? When I talk about regulatory reform in the United States, I am referring to the 235 rulemaking mandates in the Dodd-Frank Wall Street Reform and Consumer Protection Act of 2010. When I talk about global reform, I am generally referring to the new and more stringent capital, liquidity, and leverage requirements known as Basel III. Will these changes ultimately make the U.S. and global financial system safer, sounder, and more stable? Will our financial system be better able to withstand the initial stresses and subsequent contagion threats generated by extreme events?

The short answer is: It's still too early to tell.

The longer answer is: The rewriting of the rules under which financial institutions operate has the potential to be a major Stewardship success story. In fact, if it is done right, it could serve as an example of the way to address other sustainability crises we are facing.

The sustainability community clearly believes that the Dodd-Frank Act is making the world a better place. Here's what the Forum for Sustainable and Responsible Investment* said when it commented on the passage of Dodd-Frank: "The fact that financial reform accomplished many of the priorities of socially responsible and sustainable investors is [a] sign that the key principles that have been at the core of our work for years are being widely embraced. The financial markets, investors, and consumers will be better off as a result of the action taken by the Senate and the House of Representatives."[1]

Unfortunately, this more sanguine assessment of the Dodd-Frank Act has gotten lost in the shuffle.

Already Safer and Sounder

Let's start with a recap. A lot has already happened to make the U.S. financial system safer and more resilient in the last couple of years. U.S. financial institutions have raised more than $300 billion in new equity capital and have repaid U.S. taxpayers for the Troubled Asset Relief Program (TARP) investments made in 2008 and 2009—at a profit currently estimated at more than $10 billion. The largest U.S.

---

*Formerly the Social Investment Forum (SIF). The U.S. membership association for professionals, firms, institutions, and organizations engaged in socially responsible and sustainable investing. US SIF and its members advance investment practices that consider environmental, social, and corporate governance criteria to generate long-term competitive financial returns and positive societal impact (http://ussif.org/about/).

banks have reduced their leverage ratios from 16:1 to 11:1. They have increased loan loss reserves by about 200 percent. Off-balance-sheet activities have been dramatically scaled back.[2]

As U.S. Treasury Secretary Timothy Geithner wrote in July 2011, the one-year anniversary of the Dodd-Frank Act, "By almost any measure, the U.S. financial system is in much stronger shape, not just relative to the depth of the crisis but also relative to conditions that prevailed before it hit." The Secretary also stressed the reduction in leverage and greater regulatory authority in the following ways:

Less Leverage

"[B]y reducing leverage we have taken the most important step toward diminishing the risk of future crises. We have forced the largest financial institutions to take less risk and to hold much stronger financial cushions against the commitments they make."

Three Times More Capital

"Our banking regulators have reached global agreement on new capital standards that require the world's largest financial firms to hold roughly three times more capital relative to risk than before the crisis."

Limits on Nonbanks

"And for the first time, we have the ability to extend these types of limits on risk-taking to firms that may not call themselves banks but could still pose catastrophic risk to the economy were they to fail."[3]

> *"By almost any measure, the U.S. financial system is in much stronger shape, not just relative to the depth of the crisis but also relative to conditions that prevailed before it hit."*
> —U.S. Treasury Secretary Timothy Geithner

Just about everyone participating in the regulatory reform effort agrees on two things: (1) that there is a need for the global financial system to be regulated (Appendix A contains one of the most concise summaries I have ever read of the case for financial services regulation) and (2) that the regulatory infrastructure in place before 2008 and 2009 was inadequate. After all, the major pillars of that infrastructure were put into place at the beginning of the previous century. The financial system has changed dramatically since the 1920s, 1930s, and 1940s.

Going into the crisis, the U.S. financial system was governed by Depression-era laws that created our basic regulatory institutions. These 1930s institutions carried out their missions for the next 60, 70, and 80 years. In a burst of regulatory creativity, Washington invented a slew of major new government agencies that went on to form the underlying foundation of our financial markets. This 1930s infrastructure exists in pretty much the same form to this day. Consider that:

- The Securities Act of 1933 required, among other things, better disclosure by publicly held companies.
- The Banking Act of 1933 created the Federal Deposit Insurance Corporation.
- The Securities Exchange Act of 1934 created the Securities and Exchange Commission.
- The Banking Act of 1935 established the FDIC as a permanent agency of the federal government.
- The Investment Company Act of 1940 created rules for mutual funds.
- The Investment Advisers Act of 1940 created rules for advisors who provide advice for a fee, including managing client money on a discretionary basis.

Even before the crisis, there was a widely shared recognition that our financial regulatory infrastructure was in need of an update. In early 2008, U.S. Treasury Secretary Hank Paulson announced a "Blueprint for Regulatory Reform" designed to improve regulation of the U.S. financial markets.

> Our current regulatory structure was not built to address the modern financial system with its diversity of market participants, innovation, complexity of financial instruments, convergence of financial intermediaries and trading platforms, global integration and interconnectedness among financial institutions, investors and markets.[4]

Besides the fact that our modern financial markets had evolved much faster than regulators' ability to police them, Dodd-Frank and Basel III were necessary for another reason. There was and is a crying need to restore public trust and confidence. Just about everyone also agrees that the covenant between financial services firms and their clients was deeply damaged during the crisis and needs to be restored. Part of the solution needs to come through the rewriting of rules that govern the way financial institutions provide services to those clients. Consumer confidence in financial institutions has declined steadily over the past several decades, hitting a new low after the crisis, where it remains today. (See Figure 5.1.)

> *The covenant between financial services firms and their clients was deeply damaged during the crisis and needs to be restored.*

Responses to the question "If someone asked you to describe Wall Street in one word or phrase, what would you say?" are no more encouraging. (See Figure 5.2 for the answer.)

Public trust and confidence in the financial markets and in financial institutions continues to be hurt by the tremors and dislocations that keep popping up that remind traumatized investors of what they went through during the financial crisis . . . even though global equity markets have recovered since 2009. These include:

- The Flash Crash on May 6, 2010, in which the Dow Jones Industrial Average dropped 998.50 points, its biggest intraday point drop ever.[5]
- A rolling and steadily escalating sovereign debt crisis in Europe, which has rattled the bond markets and affected currencies and driven bank stocks, particularly European bank stocks, to near their lows of 2008.

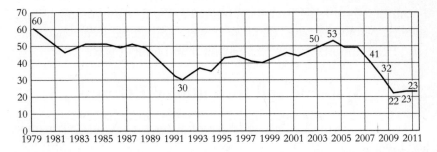

Figure 5.1 Confidence in Banks Plummets: 1979 to 2011
SOURCE: Dennis Jacobe, "Record-High 36% of Americans Lack Confidence in Banks," Gallup, June 24, 2011.

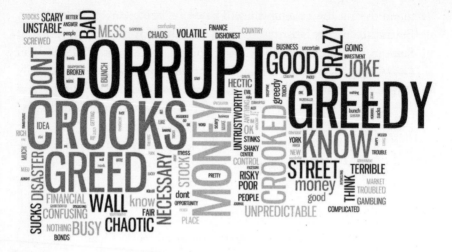

Figure 5.2   A Den of Thieves: How the Public Views Wall Street
SOURCE: The Financial Services Roundtable CEO Interview Project, Gallup, September 2010.

- The previously unimaginable spectacle of the world's greatest country, the United States, flirting in the summer of 2011 with default on more than $14 trillion of outstanding indebtedness.

"People may not know the exact details of what's going on, but when they hear that the U.S. is close to default . . . they get scared," University of Chicago finance professor Raghuram G. Rajan told the *New York Times*.[6]

Both the financial crisis itself and the lingering impact on investor confidence have created a sense of urgency and brought media attention to the underlying question: Is our financial system safe and secure? Financial reform issues have been pushed to the forefront of the political agenda. Before the crisis, these issues were considered somewhat theoretical and important only in a technical and limited way.

Systemic and Institutional Reforms

Today, efforts to update the regulatory infrastructure for financial markets and financial institutions are proceeding along two primary tracks:

1. The Basel III standards, which are new, more stringent global capital requirements, leverage restrictions, liquidity requirements, and

market—risk assessment rules. These are being developed by the Financial Stability Board (FSB) and the Basel Committee on Banking Supervision (BCBS)—with the support and backing of leaders of the G-20 developed nations.*

2. The Dodd-Frank Wall Street Reform and Consumer Protection Act, which was passed by the U.S. Congress and signed into law by President Barack Obama in July 2010. It contains some 235 rule-making mandates, and requires that 41 reports and 71 studies be completed by 11 different federal agencies and bureaus, some of which were created by the Act.

There is no way to overstate the magnitude and complexity of these combined reform efforts. They need to be coordinated across the numerous regulatory agencies that oversee the financial system in the United States, including:

Securities and Exchange Commission (SEC)
Commodity Futures Trading Commission (CFTC)
Federal Deposit Insurance Corporation (FDIC)
Financial Stability Oversight Council (FSOC)
Federal Reserve Board
Federal Trade Commission (FTC)
Consumer Financial Protection Bureau (CFPB)
Federal Housing Finance Agency (FHFA)
Government Accountability Office (GAO)
Municipal Securities Rulemaking Board (MSRB)
Office of the Comptroller of the Currency (OCC)
Office of Financial Research (OFR)
Departments of the Treasury, Agriculture, and Labor

---

*See the Glossary for complete FSB and BCBS descriptions. The Financial Stability Board was established in 2009 by the G-20 nations to coordinate central bank and financial regulatory activities across international borders. The Basel Committee on Banking Supervision provides a forum for regular cooperation on banking supervisory matters. Its objective is to enhance understanding of key supervisory issues and improve the quality of banking supervision worldwide.

These reform efforts also need to be coordinated with other countries. Global coordination is critically important because it is the only way to ensure that:

- Financial institutions don't run up against inconsistencies in the way rules are written and implemented.
- Opportunities for regulatory arbitrage are eliminated or at least largely minimized.

Without global coordination, there is the danger of greater uncertainty, reduced market efficiency, and fewer useful financial products and services because the heavier regulatory burden makes them uneconomical. Another reason global coordination is so critical is that financial institutions can respond to greater regulation by moving activities from countries where they are heavily regulated to countries where they are less so. Or activity can migrate from heavily regulated banks to more lightly regulated asset managers, hedge funds, and private equity funds that make up what is often called the shadow banking system.

The Securities Industry and Financial Markets Association (SIFMA) published Figure 5.3 to summarize the magnitude of the global financial regulatory reform challenge.

Basel Reforms

The most important elements of reform are the new requirements imposed by Basel III, particularly new capital requirements. In 2020, when we look back at this tumultuous period, that is what we will likely conclude.*

Capital is absolutely critical. It is the margin of safety that gives financial institutions the ability to recover from mistakes and to get to the other side of extended periods of severe market dislocation, when the value of assets on their balance sheets may drop quickly and sharply. It is the corporate equivalent of an individual having a comforting amount of cash in the bank when a sudden emergency occurs, whether it be a hurricane, car accident, or burglary.

---

*The history of past, current, and future Basel reforms and the place of the Basel Committee in global financial regulatory reform is summarized in Appendix B.

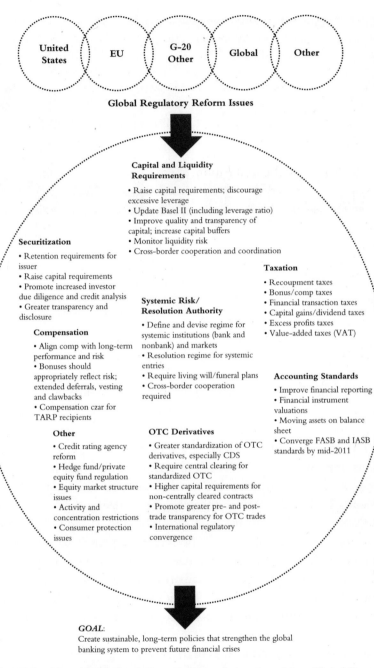

Figure 5.3 How Dodd-Frank Lays the Foundation for a New Global Financial System
SOURCE: SIFMA.

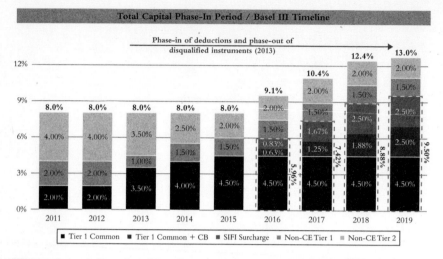

Figure 5.4 A Decade of Deadlines to Boost Bank Capital: 2011 to 2019
SOURCE: Barclays Capital Government Policy & Finance Group, BIS. Printed in and courtesy of: Jason M. Goldberg, "Outlook for the Financial Sector Implications of DFA Consumer Provisions on Banks & Bank Stocks." July 13, 2011, 9. Presented at SIFMA Regulatory Reform Summit 2011: Dodd-Frank Impact Analysis.

As we will see in Chapter 7, in a world in which financial institutions are more interconnected, extreme events have greater consequences, spread more quickly, and go deeper. In today's truly global economy, a convincing argument can be made that the need for robust capital, for a margin of safety, is greater than ever before.

The idea behind the Basel III standards is to make financial institutions more utility-like, which is to say, more like your local electrical or gas utility company—solid, stable, and reliable—and more like Canadian banks, which were the subject of Chapter 4.

These new rules were announced by the Basel Committee in September 2010. Banks were also given a phased-in schedule for complying with these new higher standards. (See Figure 5.4.) The rules require banks to hold more capital than was the case under previous international banking standards. That new capital is primarily in the form of common equity. The committee also announced higher standards for the amount of leverage that banks are allowed to have, since too many banks were far too leveraged. There are also higher standards for bank liquidity, as well as stricter rules for what constitutes capital and how to calculate risk-weighted capital.

Some highlights of Basel III capital requirements are as follows:

- The minimum Tier 1 capital ratio will be increased from 4 percent to 6 percent. Some 75 percent of this new capital must eventually be composed of common equity, which is the highest quality form of capital. Equity is the equivalent of a bank's nest egg, the rainy day money that is its backstop capital that can absorb losses if the bank stumbles.
- Starting in 2016, banks will also be required to start building up an additional capital conservation buffer composed entirely of common equity. This will have the effect of increasing minimum total capital levels to 10.5 percent by 2019.

According to *The Economist,* the net effect of all of this will be "to more than triple the amount of equity that most large banks will have to hold compared with the period before the crisis."[7] Standard & Poor's, a leading financial markets rating agency, estimates that the world's 75 largest banks will need to raise more than $750 billion in equity capital to meet these minimum thresholds. Other estimates put the total even higher, at $1.3 trillion, according to the Institute of International Finance.[8]

And that's not all. In the summer of 2011, the Basel Committee announced and confirmed that financial institutions deemed to be "globally significant" will be required to build up yet another layer of capital known as the *SIFI surcharge.* These institutions have been dubbed G-SIFIs, for Global Systemically Important Financial Institutions, and are sometimes referred to as G-SIBs, for Global Systemically Important Banks. These are the very largest financial institutions, and there are currently 29 of them, from Deutsche Bank to JPMorgan Chase. (See Table 5.1 for the complete list.)

Other Basel Reforms

While capital target ratios are the most significant of the Basel reforms, there are numerous other provisions that could have, individually and collectively, a meaningful impact on the operating models of global financial institutions. A report published in September 2011 by

Table 5.1   The Ultimate Who's Who of Financial Institutions

Bank of America	Dexia	Nordea
Bank of China	Goldman Sachs	Royal Bank of Scotland
Bank of New York Mellon	Group Crédit Agricole	Santander
Banque Populaire CdE	HSBC	Société Générale
Barclays	ING Bank	State Street
BNP Paribas	JPMorgan Chase	Sumitomo Mitsui FG
Citigroup	Lloyds Banking Group	UBS
Commerzbank	Mitsubishi UFJ FG	UniCredit Group
Credit Suisse	Mizuho FG	Wells Fargo
Deutsche Bank	Morgan Stanley	

SOURCE: Financial Stability Board, November 4, 2011.

McKinsey & Company titled "Day of Reckoning?" summarizes the most important of these as follows:[9]

Market Risk Assessment Reforms

These rules, effective at the end of 2011, increase the capital that financial institutions must hold against securities on their balance sheets, including, for example: additional capital charges based on "stressed value at risk" of all products, various new "incremental risk" and securitization charges and a "comprehensive risk measure" for certain fixed-income securities and for proprietary trading. McKinsey estimates these together could increase the capital requirements for certain securities by as much as six-fold. The point of these reforms is to make it harder for banks to get sideswiped by owning and trading credit default swaps and other derivatives, as they did in 2008 and 2009.

Rules for Capital Quality

These deduct from core capital calculations a number of forms of capital, such as capital held by insurance subsidiaries, pension fund assets, investments in other financial institutions, and deferred tax assets. This forces banks to be more transparent about the nonbanking assets on their balance sheets and to properly reserve for those activities. Again, these rules address practices that contributed to the financial crisis.

Leverage Ratio

Under this rule, effective in 2018, banks are effectively limited to lending 33 times their capital. This means banks cannot get as highly leveraged as they were during the financial crisis, when some banks were lending more than 50 times their capital.

Liquidity Coverage Ratio

This ratio, calculated by dividing a bank's highly liquid assets by "net cash flow outflow over a 30-day period," must be greater than 100 percent. Along with its companion requirement the Net Stable Funding Ratio, this requirement is designed to ensure a financial institution has adequate short-term liquidity and longer-term funding, as well as to improve the chances they could survive a run on the bank.

Counterparty Credit Risk

Capital requirements are increased, when appropriate, based on the quality of collateral and the creditworthiness of the firms a financial institution does business with. This bolsters the capital that banks must hold if they trade with a shaky entity. The idea is that if anything happens to the counterparty, the bank will have the capital cushion to absorb the trading loss and protect its deposit holders.

Dodd-Frank Act

While the Financial Stability Board and the Basel Committee are busy negotiating new capital, leverage, and liquidity rules, regulators in the United States are also extremely busy. U.S. regulators are implementing the single-largest delegation of rulemaking authority by Congress in modern history. Indeed, this job is so big and takes place over so many years, some say that regulators are overwhelmed by the task. The Dodd-Frank Act, all 2,000-plus pages of it, was signed into law by President Obama on July 21, 2010. It authorizes, and in some cases requires, federal agencies to implement 235 new rules over a five-year period, with deadlines for accomplishing most of that by the end of 2011.

I believe the following four key areas, described in descending order of importance, will be the most effective in mitigating future crises.

Systemic Oversight and Prudential Regulation

Dodd-Frank created a new federal agency, the Financial Stability Oversight Council (FSOC), to identify, monitor, and, if necessary, correct the build-up of systemic risks across the entire financial system.

This body is not just responsible for overseeing banking institutions, which was and remains the purview of the Federal Reserve, but it will also oversee the shadow banking system. The shadow banking system consists of lightly regulated financial entities like hedge funds and sovereign wealth funds that, until now, fell outside of the authority of the SEC, the Fed, and other regulators. The FSOC is actually a council of regulators, composed of the Federal Reserve, the Comptroller of the Currency, the SEC, FDIC, CFTC, FHFA, and the National Credit Union Administration Board. The chair is the secretary of the Treasury. There is also one independent member and five nonvoting members. It has the ability to draw on the data-gathering and analytical capabilities of another newly established entity, the Office of Financial Research. The FSOC is the agency responsible for coordinating Dodd-Frank rulemaking by and across federal agencies, a subject I address in more detail further on. It is responsible for seeing that the capital, leverage, and liquidity requirements in the United States are consistent with Basel III. The FSOC met for the first time in October 2010.

Systemic risk generally arises from a combination of the large size and the considerable interconnectedness of financial institutions operating in global markets. When one or more financial institutions fail, the real danger is the domino, or cascading, failure effect of those financial institutions potentially dragging down other otherwise healthy financial institutions. The best analogy is to imagine banks and financial institutions as a team of mountain climbers, roped together and scaling a rock face, with the risk that one member of the team falls and pulls the other team members down with him. It's what almost happened when Lehman Brothers declared bankruptcy, and as a result the Reserve Primary Fund broke the buck and money markets started freezing up. It's what regulators were afraid would happen if they had let the insurance company American International Group (AIG) fail in the fall of 2008.

The purpose of the Financial Stability Oversight Council is to scan the system for imbalances, excesses, bubbles, and anomalies—much as an early warning Doppler radar scans the skies for severe weather—and proactively defuse those risks before they destabilize the financial system.

Resolution Authority
Another key provision in the Dodd-Frank Act is that U.S. regulators were given new authority to resolve failing companies that pose a threat

to the nation's financial system. They can shut down, unwind, dismantle, or reorganize crippled financial institutions. The FDIC has historically had the power to resolve failing banks, but this now goes beyond banks and extends to any other type of financial institution whose problems pose a systemic threat, as determined by the FDIC, Federal Reserve, and Treasury Department. Since neither Lehman Brothers nor AIG was a bank, this is a big improvement. No government agency, including the FDIC, was authorized to wind down Lehman or AIG.

Financial institutions are now required to develop plans—so-called living wills—that provide regulators with a road map for how to best and most efficiently take the organization through a bankruptcy-like liquidation, should that become necessary.

Derivatives Reform

Dodd-Frank authorizes changes in the market for derivatives that are nothing short of transformational. The two regulatory agencies that oversee derivatives, the CFTC and the SEC, will implement these changes.

Derivatives are contracts based on underlying financial assets—such as stocks, bonds, currencies, and commodities—or on almost anything for which a reference value exists, such as interest rates or credit default data. They are most often used to manage risks by transferring exposure from one party to another. Derivatives come in many forms, including futures, forwards, over-the-counter or customized options, swaps, and credit default swaps. Users include not just financial institutions, but manufacturers, producers, distributors, and service companies that want to lock in or protect themselves, or both, against changes in the prices of commodities, interest rates, or currencies.

Before the crisis, derivative contracts were for the most part written and traded between financial institutions, all of which served as counterparties to one another. A counterparty is simply a trading partner with whom a financial institution has conducted a trade. If I sell you my old refrigerator, you are my counterparty. Warren Buffett's famous description of derivatives as "financial weapons of mass destruction" alluded to the risk that if one major counterparty failed to honor its obligations, it might render other counterparties unable to honor theirs.

For this reason, the most important derivatives-related reform required by Dodd-Frank is the obligation that standardized derivatives take a page from the futures market and be traded on regulated exchanges. They can also be traded through newly formed "swap execution facilities" and, in the case of standardized swaps, be cleared through central clearinghouses, which act as middlemen. This reduces the risk of default, namely that one party to a trade will default on its contractual obligations in a way that destabilizes the market. Swap dealers will be subject to increased capital and margin requirements and will need to disclose more trading and market-making activity to regulators on a timelier basis, thereby helping to make the derivatives market more transparent than it has been in the past.

The premise of these rules is that systemic risks posed by derivatives can be reduced by increasing transparency and transferring counterparty risk to regulated, well-capitalized exchanges and clearinghouses.

Securitization

The word *securitization* refers to the process of bundling assets, which are packaged into new securities that can be traded in financial markets. These assets are often illiquid but have predictable cash flows. Securitization is often used to fund loans that financial institutions make to their end clients, including car loans, student loans, residential and commercial mortgages, or commercial loans. Bonds backed by mortgages are generally referred to as *mortgage-backed securities* (MBS), while bonds backed by other loans are generally referred to as *asset-backed securities* (ABS). MBS whose underlying collateral deteriorated rapidly in 2008 and 2009 are viewed as one of the primary precipitators and accelerants of the financial crisis.

In an attempt to make financial institutions more accountable for the quality of underlying collateral and the performance of their MBS and ABS securitizations, Dodd–Frank imposes a risk-retention requirement on the financial institution issuing the security. This means that, with the exception of bonds backed by the highest quality residential mortgages, issuers need to retain unhedged exposure to at least 5 percent of the face value of the deals they issue. Flaws in the model of "originate to distribute," which author Satyajit Das calls "originate and hide," will be addressed by this requirement, which makes it harder for "complex chains of transactions [to allow] risk and debt to move from a place where it [is] observable to places where it [is] hidden and unregulated."[10]

There are many other reform provisions contained in Dodd–Frank, like the Volcker Rule, which prohibits banks from trading with firm money for purposes unrelated to serving clients, and the creation of a new Consumer Financial Protection Bureau to regulate mortgage lending and credit cards. These two provisions generated substantial heat, light, and noise during Congress's debate on financial reform and continued to do so during the rulemaking phase of reform.

But the reforms I've listed here—systemic oversight, resolution authority, derivatives, and securitization reform—that, if properly implemented in a balanced and careful way, have the potential to contribute meaningfully to a safer, sounder, more stable financial system. These issues may have grabbed fewer headlines, but ultimately could have a more positive long-term impact.

The Challenges of Reform

Despite the many positives, there is no shortage of challenges facing the Stewardship undertaking of financial regulatory reform. I discuss a number of them next.

To begin with, the pace of implementation has been painstakingly slow. Dodd-Frank originally called for rules to be written and reforms to be implemented over the course of two to five years, with the bulk of that work to be accomplished by the end of 2011. (See Figures 5.5 and 5.6.)

A scorecard prepared by the law firm Davis Polk & Wardwell indicates that as of December 2011, only 23 percent of the rules that were to have been finalized were finalized on schedule, with 77 percent missing their deadlines.[11]

That is not necessarily a bad thing. It may in fact be an indication that regulators are trying to get it right, and to navigate responsibly through the enormous complexity of reform. But the slow pace of reform has perpetuated uncertainty for financial services firms over the future rules they will be required to follow. Bank of America analyst Guy Moszkowski adds that prevailing uncertainty over the effect these rules may have has hampered the recovery of the capital markets.[12]

In addition to the pace of reform, coordination is a big issue: coordination across the U.S. agencies charged with reform and coordination

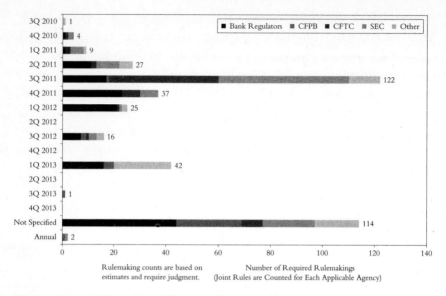

Figure 5.5 A Three-Year Blizzard of Paperwork
SOURCE: "Dodd-Frank Progress Report," Davis Polk & Wardwell LLP, December 2011.

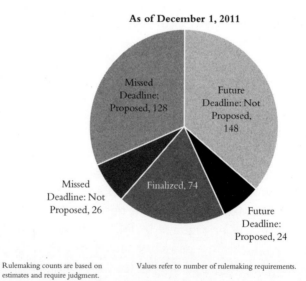

Figure 5.6 A Mountain of Regulatory Work Left To Do
SOURCE: "Dodd-Frank Progress Report," Davis Polk & Wardwell LLP, December 2011.

across the G-20 nations that are looking to implement reform on more or less the same schedule.

Regulators [must] continue to try to get it right when it comes to striking a balance between safety and growth. . . .

In areas like derivatives, for example, Dodd-Frank split responsibilities between the SEC and the CFTC. This has created numerous and not insignificant inconsistencies in the rules the two agencies have separately proposed—making it difficult for derivatives dealers to function. And the pace of derivatives reform in the United States has to this point been more aggressive than in Europe. This difference in pace threatens the ability of U.S. financial institutions to compete with their foreign counterparts in global markets.

In an even more dysfunctional display of lack of coordination, the Department of Labor (DOL) stepped in front of the SEC to propose an expansive redefinition of what it means to be a fiduciary in Employee Retirement Income Securities Act (ERISA) plans. The DOL expanded that definition for the first time to Individual Retirement Accounts before the SEC even had an opportunity to put pen to paper to write the new fiduciary standard it is authorized to apply to "personalized investment advice."

Thankfully, in the face of withering criticism, the DOL withdrew its proposed definition and application of ERISA fiduciary duty and indicated it planned to make a new proposal in early 2012.

The DOL example is important because it illustrates that for reform to be effective, "Uniform global rules and their consistent global application . . . are critical if the U.S. is to maintain its position as the deepest, most liquid, and most innovative financial market in the world," in the words of my colleague, SIFMA CEO Tim Ryan, when he testified before the House Financial Services Committee.[13]

Ryan likens the coordination challenge to landing 235 incoming airplanes at an airport, and writes:

> If the regulators do not coordinate, we will be left with a fragmented regime of conflicting or mismatched rules that could result in friction or even failures in market operations. Such friction or failures will impede the flow of capital and credit, undermining economic growth and job creation.[14]

The third challenge to effective reform is the potential migration of risky activities to the unregulated markets and unregulated institutions that compose the shadow banking system. A Morgan Stanley/Oliver Wyman report predicts:

> Markets and regulators may underestimate how much business could move into hedge funds, private equity, asset managers, and other alternative sources of capital over the long term, as banks respond to the regulatory agenda. Whilst we do not expect change to happen overnight, parts of merchant banking, direct lending, debt restructuring, proprietary trading, and parts of trading and structuring complex derivatives could migrate out of the highly regulated deposit-supported banking sector.[15]

Fourth, there are still significant gaps in regulatory infrastructure that leave the door open to destabilizing events. For example, Dodd-Frank does nothing to address the risk that money market funds like the Reserve Primary Fund might once again break the buck and trigger a crisis of confidence in the short-term money markets. Corporations, particularly financial institutions, rely on the short-term money markets to fund their ongoing operations. This issue is at least being discussed by a group called the President's Working Group on Financial Markets, and SEC chairwoman Mary Schapiro has signaled her agency's intention to introduce money market fund reforms "soon."

Similarly, Dodd-Frank is silent on issues of market structure, such as the emergence of high-speed, high-frequency, and algorithmic programs that currently dominate trading on exchanges and on unregulated electronic exchanges. While SEC chairwoman Schapiro has repeatedly stated her commitment to addressing market structure concerns, to this day, events that precipitated the 1,000-plus-point Flash Crash in May of 2010 have not been fully explained.

Finally, perhaps the biggest challenge facing reform has to do with the balance between increased safety and stability, on the one hand, and economic growth, on the other. There is no ongoing process, mechanism, or accountability for determining whether or how well that balance is or is not being achieved.

The much-vilified former U.S. Federal Reserve chairman Alan Greenspan, whom many hold responsible for the regulatory failures that led to or at least exacerbated the financial crisis, wrote a piece for the *Financial Times* in July 2011 that discusses this policy issue as articulately as anything written on the subject.

> "Since the devastating Japanese earthquake and . . . the global financial tsunami," Greenspan wrote, "governments have been pressed to guarantee their populations against . . . risks exposed by those extremely low probability events. But should they? Guarantees require the building up of a buffer of idle resources that are not otherwise engaged in the production of goods and services. They are employed only if, and when, the crisis emerges."
>
> Greenspan identifies "excess bank equity capital" as one kind of buffer "that is not otherwise available to finance productivity-enhancing capital investment" and goes on to say, "The choice of funding buffers is one of the most important decisions that societies make. . . . How much of its ongoing output should a society wish to devote to fending off once-in-50- or 100-year crises?"
>
> " . . . [A]n excess of buffers" to guarantee against risks, Greenspan writes, is possible only "at the expense of our standards of living."[16]

Increased capital requirements, leverage restrictions and liquidity restrictions in Basel III, and every one of the 235 rules in Dodd-Frank represent decisions to move chips from the economic growth side of the table over to the safety and stability side of the table. The problem is that no one is adding up the cumulative effect of this redistribution of chips on economic growth.

Clearly, the effect of Basel III and Dodd-Frank reforms will be to increase the costs for banks, brokerage firms, and other financial institutions. It will be costlier for them to do what they do best—engage in a range of activities that facilitate economic growth: lending, hedging risks, raising new debt and equity capital, and market making. Every financial sector analyst worth their salt has attempted to quantify and assess the magnitude of the impact of financial reform on bank profitability. Morgan Stanley and Oliver Wyman estimate that "New regulations will depress industry RoE [return on equity] 4 [to] 6 percent . . . "[17] (off historically high pre-crisis RoE of 17-plus percent)—mostly as a result of Basel III requirements for increased equity capital. Higher capital requirements require banks to either reprice products and services, or to cut back on or eliminate activities that are no longer able to generate returns sufficient to justify the use of more—and more expensive—capital. In either case, end users will be negatively affected. And so will economic growth.

To this point, only a couple of attempts have been made to quantify the impact of financial reform on the U.S. economy and on the global economy. One was a study by the Institute of International Finance (IIF) titled, appropriately enough, "The Cumulative Impact on the Global Economy of Changes in the Financial Regulatory Framework." The IIF study concludes that "the economic impact of . . . reforms—in terms of real GDP and employment foregone [sic]—will be significant."[18] It estimates the real level of GDP in five years will be 3.2 percent lower than it would otherwise have been; and that global employment levels will be lower by 7.5 million jobs.

The study also concludes that "this impact will be concentrated on the major mature economies, which already have a slow growth problem."[19]

Another analysis, this one by the Financial Stability Board's and Basel Committee's Macroeconomic Assessment Group (MAG), collaborating with the International Monetary Fund, forecasts a much smaller impact on the global economy. It found that Global Systemically Important Banks would raise their lending spreads to customers by an average of only 31 basis points (.31 percentage points) as a result of increased capital requirements. It also found that GDP growth would be diminished by only 4 basis points (.04 percentage points) from what it would have been without new requirements. The analysis concludes that the benefits to taxpayers from a safer financial system are "many times the costs of the reforms in terms of temporarily slower annual growth."[20]

Clearly, predicting the impact of Basel reforms is like trying to predict the weather two years into the future. It is an imprecise science at best. But that doesn't make it any less important that regulators continue to try to get it right when it comes to striking a balance between safety and growth, stability and economic recovery.

For financial regulatory reform is "like any strong medicine," former comptroller of the currency Eugene Ludwig told the Senate Banking

Committee. "[I]f applied incorrectly or excessively, the Dodd-Frank Act can produce more harm than good."[21]

Implementing reform in a way that makes the financial system safer without unduly affecting economic growth—that, in a nutshell, is the Stewardship challenge of post-crisis reform.

■ ■ ■

Interlude
Too Small to Save?

In November 2010, Bill Johnstone, the highly respected CEO of Montana-based Davidson Companies (whose holdings include D.A. Davidson, a regional brokerage firm), organized a day-long conference at the University of Minnesota Law School on the topic "Too Small to Save?" Reflecting Johnstone's laconic sense of humor, the title was an intentional parody of the phrase "Too Big to Fail," which we heard all too often during the financial crisis, and still hear today.

The premise behind the conference, he told me in an interview, was "the need to recognize and respect the value of diversity in our financial services sector—diversity in the form of small regional brokerage firms, investment advisors, and community banks. There is a societal benefit to that diversity that should be preserved."

During the financial crisis and in its wake, extraordinary resources were invested in shoring up the largest financial institutions. Yet most smaller players were left to fend for themselves.

"At smaller firms, real decision making takes place closer to what we see as our four constituencies: employees, clients, shareholders, and communities—in that order.

"If you don't serve and respect all four, ultimately you won't serve shareholders' interests. Shareholders' interests are not a corporation's only interest. If that's the focus, it leads to the problems we saw during the financial crisis. It leads to a failure of Stewardship."

Johnstone told me he believes that at smaller firms "the element of personal judgment translates more readily into business decisions."

"Leadership is ultimately about judgment and values," says Johnstone. "Let's take me versus the leader of one of the financial institutions described as 'too big to fail.' Let's suppose we have roughly the same intellectual capacity. Let's say we have the same values. Let's say our commitment to responsible Stewardship is about the same. If those things are true, then I should be better able to influence my smaller organization because I'm closer to it. Because I'm closer to facts on which decisions need to be made. Because I'm closer to our people—clients and employees.

"Many of the failures of larger financial organizations can be attributed to the inability of the leadership to translate their values and judgments and influence behavior throughout the organization. An exclusive focus on preserving large financial institutions and their concentration of power and size is not healthy. To preserve diversity and lessen risk in our financial system and economy, we must recognize and respect the value and role of our smaller firms and businesses."[22]

Chapter 6

Making the Investor Safer

In Defense of New Fiduciary Rules

Arguably the single most important investor protection issue for retail investors.

—Barbara Roper, director of investor protection at the
Consumer Federation of America, referring to
the new fiduciary standard for investment professionals

The retail brokerage business is all too frequently, and often unfairly, vilified in the media for not taking care of its clients. But in April 2009, on a conference call with brokerage industry leaders serving on the Securities Industry and Financial Markets Association's (SIFMA's) Private Client Group Steering Committee, that negative stereotype was shattered.

Culminating months of analysis and discussion, the committee, which I chaired, put to a roll call vote the question of whether or not to support a fiduciary standard of care for financial advisors who provide personalized investment advice to individual investors. Fiduciaries have a legal and moral obligation to put their clients' interests first and to disclose any conflicts of interest.

The committee members stepped up and did the right thing.

I say "the right thing" because the word *fiduciary* is viewed by investors as the gold standard in investor protection. Because it is consistent with what the best wealth management professionals already do in dealing with their clients. And because, after the crisis of 2008–2009, nothing short of the gold standard will restore investor trust and confidence in the financial markets and in our industry.

As we went down the voting roster, I actually got goose bumps hearing each of the representatives of the member firms weigh in. "Merrill Lynch supports a fiduciary standard of care." "Fidelity supports a fiduciary standard." I remember thinking: "We are witnessing a genuine inflection point in the evolution of the wealth management industry." And more importantly, "We were taking a giant step toward aligning the interests of wealth management firms with the interests of our clients."

To me, it was a prime example of Stewardship in action.

There was unanimous support that day for a fiduciary standard. While the devil is always in the details, I'm confident that it can be written in a way that preserves clients' ability to access the broad range of products and services currently offered by wealth management firms; allows clients to choose who and what kind of advisor they want to work with; and allows them to choose how they want to pay for those services (through a sales commission or a fee).

Committee members were supportive not so much because they saw the need for their business practices to change; but because best practices in the wealth management industry have evolved to the point at which they are consistent with a fiduciary standard.

Certainly, the catastrophic market events of the previous year and a half, dominating as they did the professional and personal lives of committee members, also gave us a reason to act decisively. But I'm proud to say SIFMA's support has remained strong and consistent, and has helped create momentum for what has become one of the most visible and important components of Dodd-Frank. This is a provision in Section 913 of the Act that gives the SEC the authority, but not the requirement, to write a new federal fiduciary standard of care that would apply to every investment professional who provides personalized investment advice about securities to individual investors.

Suitability versus Fiduciary Standard

No less a consumer advocate than Barbara Roper, director of investor protection at the Consumer Federation of America, calls Section 913 "arguably the single most important investor protection issue for retail investors."[1]

Roper applauds the regulators and the industry for embracing this new standard. "The SEC has come up with an approach on fiduciary duty that would preserve the broker-dealer business model and, with it, investor choice. That approach has won praise from investor advocates, state securities regulators, advisor groups, and even the major broker-dealer trade associations," says Roper.[2]

But why is this such an important issue?

Because, since the Securities Act of 1933 and the Investment Advisers Act of 1940 became law, brokers and investment advisors have been subject to different regulatory standards.

Brokers—who operate on the basis of instructions from clients and cannot exercise discretion on behalf of their clients—are subject to what is known as a *suitability standard*. Suitability, as the name suggests, means ensuring that an investment product or financial service offered to a client is suitable for that client, given their overall circumstances, including their age, financial resources, level of sophistication, and risk tolerance. Investment advisors, to whom clients give discretion to manage their money without approving each and every trade, are subject to a fiduciary standard. Both standards require advisors to put the best interests of their clients front and center when offering advice and executing transactions. But rules about disclosing and managing conflicts of interest differ between the two.

Today, as business models have converged, many wealth management advisors offer both types of services—brokerage and investment management. They work for firms that are dually registered as broker-dealers and investment advisors. And they themselves hold licenses to engage in both types of activities. They offer advice across a broad range of account types, products, and services, including:

- Public offerings of stocks, bonds, mutual funds, and exchange-traded funds.
- Secondary market trading.

- Insurance products (life, variable annuities, and long-term care).
- Mortgages and lines of credit.
- Debit and credit cards and bank deposits.
- Alternative investments (managed commodity futures, hedge funds, private equity funds).
- Trust accounts.
- Financial, retirement income, and estate plans—for individuals, households, and families.

In some of their dealings with clients, advisors need to follow suitability rules. In others, they are obligated to act as fiduciaries. Those rules are variously enforced by the SEC, the Financial Industry Regulatory Authority (FINRA), or state securities regulators, depending on the type of firm advisors work for and the type of service they are offering.

The result is more than a little confusing.

Individual investors don't understand any of this. Nor should they have to. The policy rationale behind Section 913 of Dodd-Frank is that individuals should receive the same level of protection regardless of the firm or advisor they work with or the type of product, service, or advice they receive.

But I believe there is an even more important reason for adopting a harmonized fiduciary standard of care for all types of personalized investment advice.

Economic Growth Depends on Trust

The willingness of individuals to save and invest is a critical driver of long-term economic growth. Even under the best of conditions, investing is an act of faith. Faith, as fictional White House spokesperson C. J. Cregg quotes from the Bible in the television series *The West Wing*, is "the substance of things hoped for, and the evidence of things not seen." It requires some level of conviction that if they put their savings into stocks, bonds, cash, mutual funds, ETFs, or annuities, or if they hand it over to an investment advisor to manage, the value of their investment will grow over time. As we will see in the next chapter, that tenet of investment faith, that conviction that underpins the activity of wealth management, was severely tested by the financial crisis. It was thrown into question by the lost decade of 2000 to 2010, during which U.S. stock indices moved sideways. It was shattered by the Madoff scandal and by other high profile instances of fraud and abuse. And was undermined again by the European sovereign debt and banking crisis.

The willingness of individuals to save and invest is a critical driver of long-term economic growth.

It isn't surprising that in response to the question, "Please tell me if you have a great deal, quite a lot, some, or very little trust in" businesses and organizations they deal with, respondents to a 2011 Gallup poll placed investment brokers/advisors near the bottom of the list, and banks a few notches higher. (See Figure 6.1.)

As the *New York Times* put it after the Standard & Poor's downgrade of the United States' credit rating, "The pros on Wall Street are forever telling us to keep socking our money away in that 401(k) plan and to keep believing, whatever the market's daily ups or downs. But . . . even the smart-money crowd seems to have second thoughts about the old steady-as-she-goes approach."[3]

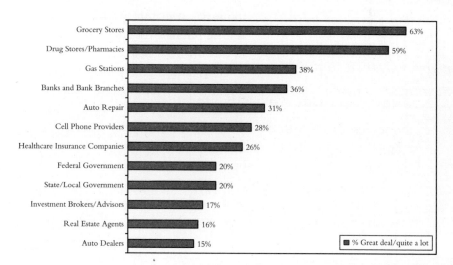

Figure 6.1 The Public Has More Confidence in Gas Station Attendants than Bankers
SOURCE: Gallup.

In this environment, if we are to promote capital formation—and if, through capital formation, we are going to jump-start economic growth—it is critical that the financial services industry do everything it can to restore public trust and confidence in financial services institutions and capital markets.

The reason a fiduciary standard is viewed by investors as the gold standard in investor protection is that fiduciaries have a legal and moral obligation to put their clients' interests first. If they have a conflict with that "client-first obligation," they need first to disclose the conflict and then get the client's consent before acting.

This is what the best wealth management professionals already do—whether they are operating as brokers under a suitability standard, or as investment advisors under a fiduciary standard.

Since that's the case, why would we not agree to act as fiduciaries, unambiguously putting our clients' interest first, at a time when so much depends on restoring trust and confidence in our industry?

> *A fiduciary standard is viewed by investors as the gold standard in investor protection [because] fiduciaries have a legal and moral obligation to put their clients' interests first.*

Shortly after Dodd-Frank was signed into law, I wrote to clients of RBC Wealth Management:

> As a leader in the financial services industry, my top priority is to restore public trust and confidence in our financial markets. To do so, I believe, our industry must address public anger over the all-too-many instances in which financial institutions lost touch with the fundamental truth underpinning the long-term sustainability of financial markets: that unless our clients prosper, nobody prospers.
>
> In my opinion, the only way the financial services industry can restore public trust and confidence is to enter into a new covenant with our clients—one based on putting client interests first.

Phrases like *obligation to clients, putting client needs first,* and *fiduciary responsibility* can seem pretty technical and obscure. But they can all be summed up in a single word: Stewardship. It is imperative for our firms to demonstrate we are taking steps to return to our Stewardship missions and values and responsibilities.

That is why I have supported—and why I continue to support—a new fiduciary standard of care for personalized investment advice.

It is also why I strongly believe that despite all the challenges and problems associated with Basel III and Dodd-Frank implementation, financial regulatory reform is a critical test of our collective commitment to Stewardship. We need to get the balance of reform right, and stay true to the vision of responsible reform—which is to make the financial system safer, sounder, more stable, and more secure without impairing the ability of financial institutions to facilitate economic growth. If we succeed, we will have demonstrated that we can successfully tackle a global issue critical to our quality of life on this planet.

Financial regulatory reform is a critical test of our collective commitment to Stewardship.

At this point, that is worth a lot.

■ ■ ■

Interlude
An Obligation of Honor

Jeff Slocum has a world-class collection of contemporary art. Yet the founder of Jeffrey Slocum & Associates also has an offbeat sense of humor. Amidst the fine art, you'll find a dayglow-on-velvet version of the kitsch art classic: Elvis with a tear running down his cheek.

In his role as a consultant to institutional and ultra high net worth investors, Slocum says he's seen "far too many" examples of financial services providers failing to live up to their Stewardship responsibilities.

"I think that's because it's an Old-World concept," Slocum told me. "When I think of Stewardship, I think of an 'obligation of honor.' That doesn't easily occur to Americans, where it's all about being the guy with the fastest gun. Being stewards doesn't come naturally to us."

Slocum recounts the behavior of a hedge fund established by the family of a prominent billionaire who managed money for family members and for third-party investors. The fund, which at one point held several billion dollars in assets, saw its assets evaporate, and was forced into liquidation to pay creditors during the height of the mortgage and liquidity crisis in 2008. Unfortunately, there was only several hundred million dollars left, causing a litigious scramble among investors and creditors to retrieve their money.

"The fund was perfectly positioned to make money," Slocum told me. "They were long AAA- and AA-rated classes of commercial mortgage-backed securities and short BBB and BB tranches. But they were leveraged and they got caught by margin calls."

"There were things the family could have done to preserve value in the fund," Slocum said. "Like a short-term injection of capital—for a few days, or weeks—that would have preserved value. They didn't have to do it. Nothing in the fund's documents required them to do it. But it would have been the right thing to do . . . for the sake of their outside investors."

Slocum was one of many CEOs, partners, and principals of financial services firms whom I reached out to in the course of writing this book. I was surprised by the extent to which they felt—as insiders and as veteran industry leaders—that the model of the financial services industry is deeply broken. I was surprised by the strength of the anger they felt at the behaviors that led to the financial crisis.

Chas Burkhart is another example. The founder of Rosemont Partners, a private equity boutique that invests in specialty investment advisory firms, Chas is perhaps the most highly networked person I know in the asset management side of our industry. He has spent decades helping money managers start and grow their businesses. Like others I interviewed, just as soon as we got through catching up on our personal lives, he launched into a rant.

"Wall Street has become a product-selling machine," he told me. "It's all about what the seller can sell; what the market can bear; what the client will buy. It should be a client-driven business, but it isn't today and long hasn't been one. Because investment banks and broker-dealers exist to make money however they can—legally, but not necessarily ethically."

As for asset management firms? "They are supposed to put their clients' interest first. They're fiduciaries, after all. But some of them consistently put their business interests first. They focus on assets under management, revenues, earnings, size, or scale. They are all in a race to become more efficient and more profitable. What happened to the integrity of client relationships? Today, relationships are consistently eroded."

"It's like watching rabid dogs. There is an arrogant imperative to win at all costs. Ethics are a far lesser concern."[4]

Chapter 7

To Investors Standing on the Wings

Prepare for the Next Crisis

[You] own the central responsibility for formulating and ensuring implementation of long-term investment policy. This responsibility cannot be delegated to investment managers. It is your job, not theirs.

—Charles D. Ellis, *Winning the Loser's Game*

I n early 2009, shortly before the U.S. equity markets hit the lows of the recent financial crisis, I met a representative of a mutual fund company who had been a passenger on US Airways Flight 1549. This was the plane piloted by Capt. Chesley Sullenberger, who pulled off an emergency landing in the Hudson River. (See Figure 7.1.) The passenger had heard the engines go quiet and heard the pilot come on the intercom. He had thought his last thoughts as he braced for impact. And, when it was all over, and he stood out on the wing with the

Figure 7.1   Miracle on the Hudson
SOURCE: Associated Press.

freezing water lapping at his feet, passengers screaming, he realized . . .
he had survived.

It occurred to me then that his experience was an analogy for what
many individual investors went through during the fall of 2008 and the
spring of 2009: an emergency landing of our collective wealth management airplane. The first real hint of trouble came when Bear Stearns
failed in March of 2008. Then, the week Lehman Brothers declared
bankruptcy and the Reserve Primary Fund broke the buck, came the
realization that something was in fact very, very wrong. Next came
the feeling after September 15, 2008—which lasted for over a
year, through the following October and November—that we were in
a free fall, and potentially about to crash.

Back in March 2009, we were all standing on the airplane's wings,
figuratively speaking. (See Figure 7.2.) We were shaken and dazed and
confused. We were surrounded by an unbelievable mess. We were still
plenty worried—about fire breaking out or the plane sinking. Our plans
and our schedules were turned upside down, and we didn't have a clue
about how we were going to get to where we thought we were headed
just a short time ago.

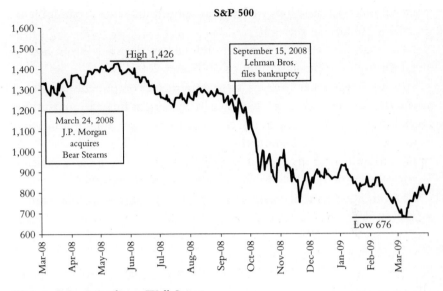

Figure 7.2 Miracle on Wall Street

Source: RBC Wealth Management-U.S. Research.

Data Source: Bloomberg stats, event dates from St. Louis Fed, "The Financial Crisis: A Timeline of Events and Policy Actions," February 27, 2007.

But we were pretty sure we were going to survive.

It turned out the fall of 2008 and winter of 2009 was an emergency landing, not a crash landing.

Like the passengers on US Airways Flight 1549, we experienced an extreme event that left us all traumatized, to one degree or another. Many of us have yet to fully recover. We were all exposed to a near-death experience, were all allowed to stare into the possibility of disaster. This nightmare was the very real possibility of a complete economic meltdown of the global financial system and, with it, the global economy. And like the passengers on the wings of the plane floating in the Hudson River, we have all been given, so to speak, another chance to change our behavior based on that extreme experience.

The Gift of a Glimpse

We should treat that as a gift. And if we are, as Charley Ellis suggests, stewards of our personal wealth and ultimately accountable for our personal financial situation, we have an opportunity and a responsibility to take advantage of that gift.

So what did we learn—what should we have learned—from having lived through the financial crisis of 2008 and 2009?

As we saw earlier, one of most important components of global financial reform is to require systemically important financial institutions to hold more core capital in reserve, and to be more liquid going forward than they were before the financial crisis. The same principle applies to individual investors in a world where *black swans* and extreme market volatility are likely going to be ongoing facts of life.

During the financial crisis, we were offered a glimpse of the fragility of the modern financial system and the global economy, which, it turns out, is more vulnerable than ever to unexpected shocks because of its complexity and interconnectedness.

We were offered a glimpse into the fact that reality is more random than we would like to admit. We saw that extreme events really can and do happen. We learned that as much as the media and politicians and regulators predictably play the "should have," "could have," and "ought to have" blame game afterward, it didn't matter. As much as we knew that housing prices were inflated, as much as we knew that risk was underpriced, that financial firms were overly leveraged and were using that leverage to load up on illiquid assets, some of them on the balance sheet but most of them in opaque, special-purpose vehicles . . . it all didn't matter. Extreme events like credit bubbles often cannot be foreseen or predicted. Even if foreseen or predicted, they cannot always be avoided.

> *During the financial crisis, we were offered a glimpse of the fragility of the modern financial system and the global economy, which, it turns out, is more vulnerable than ever to unexpected shocks because of its complexity and interconnectedness.*

The Black Swan, by Nassim Nicholas Taleb, in my opinion, is one of the most important books individual investors can read in the wake of the financial crisis of 2008–2009. Taleb writes about the importance of "black swans"—rare events whose impact is extreme and which cannot be prospectively predicted, but which can be retrospectively explained.

Taleb believes the frequency and impact of black swans has been increasing, and is likely to continue to do so.

"It started accelerating during the Industrial Revolution, as the world started getting more complicated, while ordinary events, the ones we study and discuss and try to predict from reading the newspapers, have become increasingly inconsequential," Taleb writes. "The future will be increasingly less predictable."[1]

Taleb cites an apocryphal saying attributed to Yogi Berra, "The future ain't what it used to be" and goes on to agree with him: "Gains in our ability to model (and predict) the world may be dwarfed by the increases in its complexity—implying a greater and greater role for the unpredicted." Not only that, Taleb tells us that the more important the event, the less likely we will be able to predict it.[2]

In a world in which we are "blind to randomness," Taleb suggests that "we cannot truly plan, because we do not understand the future." "But," he adds, "this is not necessarily bad news. We could plan *while bearing in mind such limitations.*[3]

"What you should avoid is unnecessary dependence on large-scale harmful predictions. . . . Be prepared for all relevant eventualities.[4] "Black swans being unpredictable, we need to adjust to their existence (rather than naïvely try to predict them)."[5]

Not only are black swans unpredictable, not only are they increasing in frequency (see Table 7.1), their consequences are more dramatic today than they have ever been, because of the interconnectedness of the world's financial institutions and the global nature of our economy.

As Taleb writes, "Globalization creates interlocking fragility, while . . . giving the appearance of stability. In other words it creates devastating black swans. We have never before lived under the threat of a global collapse."[6]

The Four Horsemen

Taleb is not the only one who has a highly relevant message in the wake of the crisis. The other book I recommend for individual investors, particularly those with a fondness for history, is Barton Biggs's *Wealth, War & Wisdom*.

Table 7.1 Another Decade, Another Crisis

Episode	Type	Global Financial Center(s) Most Affected	At Least Two Distinct Regions	Number of Countries in Each Region
The crisis of 1825–1826	Global	United Kingdom	Europe and Latin America	Greece and Portugal defaulted, as did practically all of newly independent Latin America.
The panic of 1907	Global	United States	Europe, Asia, and Latin America	Notably France, Italy, Japan, Mexico, and Chile suffered from banking panics.
The Great Depression, 1929–1938	Global	United States and France	All regions	Widespread defaults and banking crises across all regions.
Debt crisis of the 1980s	Multicountry (developing countries and emerging markets)	United States (affected, but crisis was not systemic)	Developing countries in Africa, Latin America, and, to a lesser extent, Asia	Sovereign default, currency crashes, and high inflation were rampant.

The Asian crisis of 1997–1998	Multicountry, extending beyond Asia in 1998	Japan (affected, but by then it was five years into the resolution of its own systemic banking crisis)	Asia, Europe, and Latin America	Affected Southeast Asia initially. By 1998, Russia, Ukraine, Colombia, and Brazil were affected.
The Global Contraction of 2008	Global	United States, United Kingdom	All regions	Banking crises proliferated in Europe, and stock market and currency crashes versus the dollar cut across regions.

SOURCE: Carmen M. Reinhart and Kenneth S. Rogoff, *This Time Is Different*. Reprinted by permission of Princeton University Press.

After studying World War II and the effects it had on personal wealth, Biggs concluded that, "Wealth destruction . . . has been endemic to mankind."[7]

> For those who have wealth, it is well to always bear in mind that inevitably there will be another plague, "a time of cholera," that the Four Horsemen will ride again, and that someday, suddenly, *the barbarians* will be at your gate.[8]

In other words, "Anticipate the anticipation of trouble."[9]

The importance of preparing for extreme events—"anticipating the anticipation of trouble"—is, in my opinion, the single most important thing we, as stewards of our personal wealth, should be doing differently in the future, based on the experience we all just had of surviving the emergency landing of our metaphorical wealth management airplane.

> *"Anticipate the anticipation of trouble."*
>
> —Barton Biggs

Here are four principles for being prepared for the worst-case scenario:

1. Have a plan for dealing with the effects of extreme emotions.
2. Build a bigger safety cushion or margin of error into the management of your personal wealth.
3. Build a fortress-like cash and liquidity position.
4. Diversify against extreme events.

Step One: Make a Plan for Dealing with the Effects of Extreme Emotions

In 2008 and 2009, many of us saw how, during periods of extreme dislocation, emotionality can literally paralyze us. It can prevent us from acting either to manage risk or to take advantage of investment opportunities.

As the head of one of the largest wealth management firms in the United States, I found myself speaking during that historically volatile period to thousands of individual clients and employees about how they were reacting to the crisis. These conversations, more often than not, either started with or got around to what sleeping medications, such as Ambien or Lunesta, were most effective. I saw how desperately people wanted to connect with others who were going through the same thing. I saw how much they wanted to be able to share what and how they were feeling. I saw how hungry they were for comfort, guidance, reassurance . . . anything that could help them get their bearings back and stand, once again, on solid ground. Speaking to rooms crowded with worried investors, I found people nodding their heads whenever I would put words to the emotions they were feeling—*fear, panic, confusion*. . . . Simply naming those emotions seemed to provide some measure of relief and comfort. After I wrote and RBC Wealth Management distributed a white paper titled *Creating a Clear Path Forward*,[10] one of our employees returned from a family visit to India to tell me that a member of his family found the message of that piece so comforting and inspiring they had tacked a copy of it to their office wall.

The financial crisis reminded us how important it is to develop a plan for dealing with the extreme emotionality that is generated by severe market dislocations. Particularly when you consider that as bad as things got in 2008 and 2009, the world has served up periods of social disruption and market volatility way beyond anything we just experienced. We need only read Biggs's *Wealth, War & Wisdom* to remind ourselves that unlike European families of wealth during World War II, we weren't sewing jewelry into our children's winter coats or burying our silver in the backyard during the winter of 2008 and 2009. The −56 percent peak-to-trough drop in the value of the S&P 500 in 2008 and 2009 might have seemed like the end of the world. But it paled in comparison to its −89 percent drop in value during the Great Depression.

Jeremy Grantham, one of the most experienced and insightful investment professionals, wrote in his quarterly newsletter under the title "Reinvesting When Terrified," about the need to have a "break the glass" emergency plan for when markets are playing havoc with your emotions.

"There is only one cure for terminal paralysis: You absolutely must have a battle plan . . . and stick to it."[11]

"There is only one cure for terminal paralysis: You absolutely must have a battle plan . . . and stick to it."

—Jeremy Grantham

Because of the dynamic we saw at RBC Wealth Management—where clients were paralyzed by strong and primitive emotions during the early stages of the crisis—we developed a process and set of support materials that enabled our financial advisors to help their clients move through emotionality, to action. We branded that process RBC's *Personal Economic Recovery Strategy (PERS).*

As Figure 7.3 illustrates, PERS provided a step-by-step approach for financial advisors to use in discussions with clients to help them regain control of their feelings and make cool-headed decisions.

The two PERS steps of *Assess* and *Stabilize* are an ideal way to carry out the first principle, which is to learn how to deal with extreme emotion. The first PERS step, *Assess*, was all about helping clients put a solid emotional floor beneath their feet. PERS encouraged financial

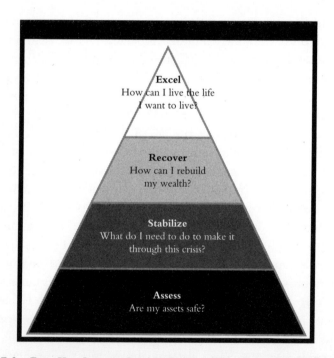

Figure 7.3 Four Key Steps to Smarter Financial Decisions: The PERS Pyramid
SOURCE: RBC Wealth Management-U.S.

advisors to contact clients with the sole objective of listening to them, without an agenda, and without preconceived ideas, paying attention to their emotions. Advisors needed to understand what clients were afraid of, worried about, okay with—so they could offer good solutions to meet their needs. These were often issues that did not involve their investment portfolio, but had an impact on their short- or long-term plans. Like concern over a son or daughter who had been laid off. Concern for a retired parent who now, as a result of diminished resources, needed additional financial support. The ripple effects of the economic meltdown created some very significant life changes for many people.

By exploring how clients felt about their investments, the markets, and the overall economy, our advisors were able to help clients end the sensation of free fall and mitigate the associated feelings of panic that may have been paralyzing them. The PERS pyramid represented a framework, a plan, for clients to start thinking about how to navigate through the crisis.

The *Stabilize* step of PERS was about helping clients begin responding to the dramatically changed, confusing, and uncertain circumstances in the world around them. One of the accepted maxims of personal investing is, "*When in doubt, do nothing.*" Which is pretty good advice in normal markets. But during markets as volatile as those of 2008 and 2009, it needs to be paired with a companion maxim: "*When paralyzed by doubt, do something.*" In my own case, "doing something" involved harvesting losses created by declining values in my investment portfolio . . . without changing my exposure to the markets. This created value by warehousing losses that could shelter future gains, when and if the markets recovered. I also drew down lines of credit, to pre-empt the possibility that those lines would be called or capped. (More on this later in this chapter.) Neither of these represented significant adjustments to my finances, but they were action steps that got me off the dime, so to speak.

Only after dealing with emotions, only after moving from paralysis to action, were individual investors able to start thinking about how to take advantage of the truly once-in-a-lifetime investment opportunities created by dislocations in the market: like convertible bonds in the late fall of 2008. Or bank preferred stocks in the winter of 2009. Or high-quality stocks in the spring and summer of 2009. The *Assess* and *Stabilize* stages of PERS were necessary portals through which individual investors needed to pass in order to take advantage of the *Recover* and *Excel* stages of the financial crisis.

Step Two: Build a Bigger Safety Cushion

In addition to having a plan to deal with extreme emotions, individual investors need to build financial positions preemptively, before the next black swan arrives. These financial positions are more readily defensible against, and in the face of, extreme market volatility than most of us had in place going into the last crisis.

Because, like it or not, we will very probably have to deal with extreme market conditions again during our lifetimes.

Any reader who wants to stay awake at night thinking about what those extreme events might look like should consider reading 7 *Deadly Scenarios*, by Andrew Krepinevich. Consider the following extreme events and the effect each will have on your investment portfolio:

1. Pakistan's collapse leads to a hunt for its nuclear weapons.
2. Major U.S. cities are leveled by black-market nukes.
3. A global pandemic finds millions swarming across the U.S. border.
4. A nuclear-armed Iran tempts war with Israel.
5. China's growing civil unrest ignites a global shutdown.
6. Terrorists manage to disrupt the world's supply of oil.
7. Muslim extremists, Iran, Russia, or even China threaten to take over in Iraq after U.S. troops pull out.[12]

Even those seven deadly scenarios aren't true black swan events, because sitting here, today, we can predict and describe them. With true black swans, "the happening and timing . . . are utterly unforecastable."[13] True black swans "make what you don't know far more important that what you do know," writes Taleb. They are "caused and exacerbated *by their being unexpected*."[14]

How, then, do individuals construct financial positions and wealth management strategies that will survive deadly scenarios or black swans?

First and foremost among the seven immutable laws of investing developed by Grantham, Mayo, Van Otterloo & Co. LLC (GMO), an investment advisory firm, is this one: "Always insist on a margin of safety."[15] This means, among other things, not flying so close to the sun when it comes to the risk-and-return trade-off in one's portfolio.

During the most recent financial crisis, I learned that my emotional tolerance for loss is less than my intellectual tolerance for loss. A negative 30 percent portfolio return (meaning a one-third reduction in the value of one's investable assets) looks a lot different on the risk tolerance questionnaires one fills out when completing a financial plan or opening a brokerage account than it does when it shows up on monthly brokerage statements and portfolio reports, as was the case in the fall of 2008. When deciding which club to use to hit their next shot, amateur golfers are advised to take one club more than they think they will need. That way, they'll swing easier and stay within their actual ability to execute a shot and make fewer mistakes that get them into trouble. The same rule holds true for investors. Our optimal asset allocation may be a notch or two less aggressive, in terms of the risk-and-return trade-offs, from what asset allocation models tell you it should be.

After the markets had stabilized in 2009, I went through a gut check exercise with my financial advisor that consisted of reviewing the portfolio results that I might experience with different asset allocation strategies—and matching them up with my recently tested understanding of what my tolerance for risk really is.

During the most recent financial crisis, I learned that my emotional tolerance for loss is less than my intellectual tolerance for loss.

We ended up dialing back the risk levels of my portfolio to a mix of assets that would have generated a maximum one-year loss of 25 percent (based on return data from the period 1926 to 2010) to one that would have generated a maximum loss of about 18 percent. That might not seem like a lot on paper, but in the midst of a financial crisis like that of 2008 and 2009, it could mean the difference between having the emotional staying power to ride out the crisis, and capitulation, meaning the unnecessary liquidation of portfolio securities for a partial or complete realized loss.

Step Three: Build a Fortress-Like Cash
and Liquidity Position

Quite frankly, many investors going into 2008 and 2009 were worrying about the wrong things in their investment portfolios. They spent time focusing on tactical tweaks—like whether to add more large cap equity exposure, small cap equity exposure, or more exposure to value stocks versus growth stocks. Instead, they would have been much better served by addressing basic, fundamental concerns like: "Do I have enough liquidity to make it through a market meltdown?" I mean, actually: "Do I have a way to pay my day-to-day living expenses for a couple of years if the credit markets freeze up and stay frozen?"

Shareholders in the Reserve Primary Fund who found themselves unable to get their hands on their money market cash for months learned the importance of diversifying across multiple sources of cash the hard way. The same goes for lines of credit. During the crisis, many banks capped or canceled lines of credit that individuals and small businesses had counted on to meet cash flow needs.

History tells us we will recover from market dislocations. As the saying goes: "The end of the world only comes once . . . and this isn't it." By March 2011, the S&P 500 had recovered 100 percent of its pre-crisis value. (See Figure 7.4.)

But to recover from a crisis, you have to survive the crisis . . . which means having access to liquid sources of enough cash to pay for years (possibly) of living expenses.

Warren Buffett is perhaps the most articulate advocate, and the most disciplined practitioner, of the fortress approach to liquidity management for his company, Berkshire Hathaway. In his 2008 letter to shareholders, he listed first among the four goals he and his partner, Charlie Munger, focus on, as "maintaining Berkshire [Hathaway's] Gibraltar-like financial position, which features huge amounts of excess liquidity, near-term obligations that are modest, and dozens of sources of earnings and cash."[16]

In 2010, Buffett wrote to shareholders that "the fundamental principle of auto racing is that to finish first, you must first finish."

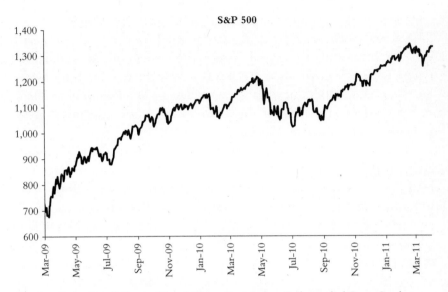

S&P 500

Figure 7.4 Don't Leave Now! How the Market Rebounded Post-Crash
SOURCE: RBC Wealth Management-U.S. Research.
DATA SOURCE: Bloomberg.

Buffett went on to describe a letter from his grandfather, Ernest, to his father and his siblings. Buffett wrote:

> Ernest never went to business school—he never in fact finished high school—but he understood the importance of liquidity as a condition for *assured* survival. At Berkshire, we . . . have pledged that we will hold at least $10 billion of cash. . . . Because of that commitment, we customarily keep at least $20 billion on hand. . . .
>
> We keep our cash largely in U.S. Treasury bills and avoid other short-term securities yielding a few more basis points, a policy we adhered to long before the frailties of commercial paper and money market funds became apparent in September 2008. . . . We don't rely on bank lines. . . .[17]

During the height of the financial crisis, Buffett wrote two checks on Berkshire Hathaway's account to buy $5 billion of preferred stock in Goldman Sachs and $3 billion in General Electric. In the fall of 2011, at the height of concerns about European sovereign debt, European banks, and the future of the euro currency, he did it again—investing $5 billion in preferred stock issued by Bank of America. Like many other observers, I marvel at Buffett's nerves of steel at times when the global financial system is melting down. Not that it was an easy thing to do, but it was a lot easier because Berkshire Hathaway still had $24.3 billion in cash and cash equivalents at the end of 2008, after making those two investments in Goldman and General Electric.[18]

The same principles that Buffett follows and that are important components of global financial reform—of holding more reserves and being more liquid—apply to individual investors as well. Both institutions and individuals are now living in a world in which black swans and extreme market volatility are likely going to be ongoing facts of life.

Leverage levels are also critical to surviving a crisis. One of the reasons so many financial institutions failed during the financial crisis is that they were carrying historically high levels of leverage. U.S. financial services debt increased from 34 percent of GDP in 1983 to 96 percent of GDP in 2003. By 2009, that percentage had risen to 120 percent.[19]

Institutions and individuals are now living in a world in which black swans and extreme market volatility are . . . ongoing facts of life.

As we saw in Chapter 4, one of the reasons Canadian banks weathered the storm was their relatively low levels of leverage. A key component of financial regulatory reform requires banks to limit the amount of leverage financial institutions can incur going forward. Once again, the same principle holds true for individuals. Another immutable law of investing from Grantham, Mayo, Van Otterloo (GMO) is "be leery of leverage."[20]

Step Four: Diversify against Extreme Events

Like most investors going into 2008 and 2009, I was well diversified across conventional asset classes—stocks, bonds, cash, real estate— and across sectors within the equity asset class—large cap stocks, mid cap stocks and small cap stocks; value- and growth-oriented investment styles; international as well as U.S. companies. But, like most investors,

I had not really diversified in a way that afforded effective insurance against a black swan event.

One of the theoretical benefits of diversification—of putting one's eggs into multiple baskets—is taking advantage of the fact that different asset classes have historically tended to behave differently from one another—at least under normal conditions and over long periods of time. To put it in more technical terms, the correlation of stocks and bonds and cash and hard assets is substantially less than 1.0.

- Stocks do better in periods of economic growth.
- Bonds protect against slow growth and deflationary environments.
- Commodities and hard assets can protect against sudden bouts of inflation.

The problem is that while conventional diversification is helpful in preserving portfolio values under normal conditions and over time, it often doesn't help when it comes to surviving a crisis. One thing that often occurs during periods of extreme market volatility is that conventional asset classes tend to act in concert . . . in the short term. This most certainly occurred during the financial crisis of 2008–2009. (See Figure 7.5.) They all tend to decline in value. During a crisis, this is what it means when you hear the technical phrase, about "correlations going to 1.0."

Here's one of the most important recommendations Biggs makes after studying the performance of different asset classes during World War II. He advises wealthy individuals to move at least a small percentage of their funds, say 5 percent, out of their primary country of residence and into an uncorrelated currency. In addition, Biggs recommends investing another 5 percent in the most indestructible of assets—arable land.

"What can you do?" asks Biggs. "In simplest terms . . . diversify your fortune both as to asset class and location."[21]

Achieving diversification by transferring money out of lucrative, *in-country* investments to sterile assets in a . . . haven is wrenching and very expensive but it has to be viewed as catastrophe insurance. No matter how safe your home country appears, even if it's the United States, every truly wealthy person should have some assets elsewhere. History suggests that nothing

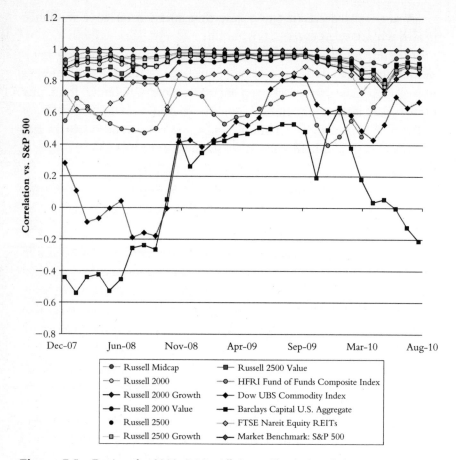

Figure 7.5 During the 2008 Crisis, All Asset Classes Acted the Same
SOURCE: RBC Wealth Management-U.S. Research.
DATA SOURCE: Zephyr Associates.

is forever. Extreme political change, a terrorist attack, a melt-down of the financial system can happen anywhere. Currency diversification is also essential.[22]

Whether Biggs's recommendations are precisely the right strategies or not, the point is that going forward, individual investors should be focusing more on true disaster insurance. As investor Jeremy Grantham tells us, "[T]he only things that really matter in investing are the bubbles and the busts."[23]

That insight is one of the gifts we were given by the financial crisis.

If land or farmland seems too lumpy, inconvenient, or illiquid an investment, then gold might suffice. But make sure to own it in physical form, and consider safekeeping it in a country outside the United States. With the public finances and fiscal policy of the United States as unsustainably out of balance as they are today, with trillion-dollar deficits stretching out as far as the eye can see, the status of the U.S. dollar as the world's reserve currency is at risk. A significant devaluation of the dollar against other currencies is plausible over the next couple of decades. This situation would increase the cost of living for anyone whose wealth is denominated in U.S. dollars, which is why owning a basket of foreign currencies is attractive as a form of disaster insurance.

Preparing better for extreme events—whether they are bubbles, busts, deadly scenarios, or other kinds of black swans—is the single most important thing that we as individual investors can do to become better stewards of our personal wealth. Quite frankly, most of us were not well prepared for these events heading into and going through 2008 and 2009.

Strategies for being prepared are simple and straightforward and have as much to do with common sense as anything else. They include dialing down the riskiness of your portfolio; reducing debt levels; building up and diversifying across sources of liquidity; and buying disaster insurance through unconventional diversification strategies.

Those are all ways to "anticipate the anticipation of trouble;" a type of trouble that is going to occur at least as often, if not more so, than it has in the past.

Something else is required to better prepare for and increase one's chances of surviving the financial consequences of a black swan event.

Individual investors need to have a deep and abiding sense of conviction about the strategy and plan that they have put into place for managing their wealth. Because conviction is what is required when we go through periods of extreme volatility as gut-wrenching as those in 2008 and 2009. We watched the Dow Jones Industrial Average drop 777.68 points in a day and 1874.19 points in a week. We need conviction to stick to and not deviate from or abandon our wealth management strategy and plan. Investors need to build their financial plan on a foundation of beliefs so fundamental that they are able to remain true to that plan no matter what alarming stories they are reading in the financial media.

During the height of the financial crisis, I wrote the following to clients of RBC Wealth Management:

> I've learned I have certain core beliefs and convictions about how the financial markets operate—like mean reversion, like the predictability of asset classes over long periods of time, like the value of diversification, in spite of the media's harping about the failure of modern portfolio theory and about there being "no place to hide." I keep repeating these beliefs to myself like some kind of wealth management version of the Lord's Prayer. In the process, I'm learning that as long as I act on the basis of those core beliefs, not only am I willing to accept the consequences, to go down with the plane, so to speak, but I actually feel better, more in control, than I do just watching the crisis unfold.

What do you believe in so strongly that you are willing to accept the consequences if you are wrong? What do you believe in so strongly that you are prepared to go down with the plane, so to speak? Less than three years after the failure of Bear Stearns, the resiliency of capital markets has been proven once again. But at the height of the crisis, it took an act of faith, of conviction, to act as if the markets would redeem themselves.

This is the quality of *purposefulness* that we identified in Chapter 3 as one of the qualities of effective Stewardship. It's worth thinking about how other Stewardship qualities can help better prepare you to deal with future extreme events.

Like *accountability*—taking seriously your responsibilities as a steward of your personal wealth and recognizing that, ultimately, you alone are responsible for how your wealth is managed.

Or *humility*—recognizing that while you are ultimately accountable, you can't execute a wealth management strategy alone. Most people, particularly those who aren't active in the financial markets every day, need to draw on the expertise of financial advisors and other experts. Particularly when the range and complexity of products and services available to individual investors is as bewildering as it is today. Particularly when the best investment opportunities are not always in our backyards, but global. And particularly when the wealth management challenges we are trying to solve are more complex than they have ever been. Very few individuals have the sophistication, on their own, to put into place today all the solutions and structures required to be prudent stewards of their own wealth.

Or the quality of *foresight*—"anticipating the anticipation of trouble," as Barton Biggs puts it.

Or, finally, *integrity*. Intellectual honesty is essential to effective management of one's financial affairs. In the context of this chapter, that means recognizing that it is impossible to predict, and impossible to avoid, black swan events. Thinking that you can avoid them or thinking you should have been able to avoid them is actually the worst lesson one can draw from the financial crisis. Continuing to believe that you can avoid or predict future crises is the best way to ensure the next crisis will be even more wealth-destroying than the last.

In his account of US Airways Flight 1549, *Highest Duty: My Search for What Really Matters,* the pilot, Captain Chesley Sullenberger, finds a waterlogged fortune from a Chinese cookie in one of four cardboard boxes of personal effects returned to him by investigators four months after the flight. The fortune reads, "A delay is better than a disaster." It reminds him of a question his daughter once asked him, "What does integrity mean?" To which he remembers answering, "Integrity means doing the right thing even when it's not convenient."

"Integrity," writes Sullenberger, "is the core of my profession. An airline pilot has to do the right thing every time. I call it a daily devotion to duty. It's serving a cause greater than ourselves."

"We need to do the right thing every time."[24]

> *"Integrity is the core of my profession. An airline pilot has to do the right thing every time. . . . It's serving a cause greater than ourselves."*
>
> —Captain Chesley Sullenberger

How interesting that the man responsible for piloting 155 people to safety on the chilly waters of the Hudson River talks in his memoirs about "serving others" and "integrity" and "doing the right thing every time" and "devotion to duty" in a book about *What Really Matters.*

Flight 1549 lasted five minutes and eight seconds. Not months; not years. The black swan cause of that particular emergency was birds hitting jet engines (something that has a 1 in 10,000 chance of happening). Not subprime mortgages. Not excessive leverage. It affected passengers on an airplane. Not investors with wealth management portfolios.

Yet what saved the lives of those 155 people was the same thing that will save us when the next financial dislocation strikes. What will save us is strong Stewardship values as lived out and described by a man who has always believed to his very core that his role in life was "to serve the world well."

■ ■ ■

Interlude
Predatory Volatility

The extreme volatility caused by fast electronic trading firms scares and confuses individual investors, who are the lifeblood of our business. As a broker in the trenches, I hear this daily. Yesterday was a perfect case in point. The market traversed over 400 Dow points in the course of the day, with a lot of that swing in the last few minutes of trading. Many investors simply don't understand how the world can be coming to an end, and then minutes later, everything seems rosy. We are losing investors who feel the deck is stacked against them. The equity markets are no longer a place for companies to raise capital and investors to participate in the growth of America's great companies, but rather a giant casino without the free drinks.

—E-mail from financial advisor

The world is a scary place these days. The year 2011 saw a Japanese tsunami and nuclear reactor crisis, the downgrading of the U.S. Treasury Bond rating to AA+, a progressively worsening European sovereign debt crisis, and four days in a row in August 2011 when the Dow Jones Industrial Average moved more than 400 points, the first time this had happened in the 115-year history of the DJIA. Psychologist Paul Slovic, of Decision Research, found that the mood of investors is at least as bad as it was in 2009. "When asked if they 'worried about money yesterday,' 73 percent said 'yes'—up from 56 percent two and one-half years ago," reported the *Wall Street Journal*.[25]

CNBC television personality Jim Cramer expressed the frustrations of mom-and-pop investors when he wrote, "We just want nothing. We don't want up. We don't want down. . . . We just want calm. I am a huge believer that these gyrations [in the stock and bond markets] . . . are awful for individual investors. . . . The velocity of the declines is very daunting. . . . [T]he SEC should make a study about why the individual

(Continued)

investor keeps leaving stocks. They will learn that it is, in part, because of these swings, which make it impossible for many people to hang on."[26]

In my role, I receive hundreds of e-mails a year from financial advisors raising issues they feel are important to their clients. A 30-year veteran in our Boulder, Colorado, office wrote that "the average investor is scared to death by the volatility of the current investment environment and is frozen into inactivity." The advisor lamented "the shearing of the sheep that are the middle-class, blue-collar workers who are trying to save for their kids' college education and retirement and who, with bonds offering little or no returns, are forced into the stock market."

The source of this increased stock market volatility is not entirely clear. But questions about the potential contributing role of so-called high-frequency trading—computer-driven algorithmic trading strategies that currently make up an estimated 60 percent of the volume on the New York Stock Exchange—show just how skeptical investors have become about participating in the capital markets.

"High Frequency Traders Manipulating the Nasty Sell-Off?" asked one headline on CNBC.[27]

"The days of you trying to make a buck actively trading in the stock market are over," opines a *Reuters Money* blogger. "Individuals don't stand a chance anymore because they are largely competing against rational machines."[28]

Retired RBC investment strategist Phil Dow recently described what he sees as a state of affairs in which "investors' serious retirement money still stands at a distinct disadvantage to the predatory volatility driven by today's high-frequency and hedged stock market operators."[29]

Here's how yet another financial advisor expressed similar concerns: "Regulators are routinely behind the curve, while the house they are charged with protecting is burning down. Little wonder there's no confidence in the markets or the regulators.

With the benefit of 32 years of experience in every market environment imaginable, I feel we are at a crucial juncture. At risk is the alienation of a large swath of investors to the detriment of themselves and our industry." A Phoenix investor put it this way: "The market cannot afford to drive out all the individual investors and it behooves the investment fraternity to first recognize that there may be a problem, and then to figure out a way to keep a two-way dialogue going with all classes of investors."

Last summer, the SEC subpoenaed executives of high-speed trading firms to determine their impact during periods of market stress and approved a "large trader" rule requiring more disclosure by high-speed traders. Shortly thereafter, the Financial Industry Regulatory Authority (FINRA) and several exchanges released rules outlining the operation of market-wide circuit breakers designed to dampen extreme volatility. The *New York Times* reported that at least one commissioner at the Commodity Futures Trading Commission (CFTC) called for registration of high-frequency trading firms and testing of their trading algorithms. But given the degree of mistrust and suspicion that exists toward financial markets, regulators will need to do even more before investors feel confident enough again to provide the kind of stable capital that is necessary for long-term economic growth.[30]

Chapter 8

Environmental, Social, and Governance Investing

Could It Be the Answer?

The world is more complicated and interconnected. ESG matters.
—Christopher Ailman, chief investment officer, California
State Teachers' Retirement System

R econnecting leaders of our financial institutions with their
Stewardship missions, values, and responsibilities is the key to
mitigating the breadth, scope, and duration of future financial
crises. That's the good news. But how do we get that to happen? It's
fine for Margaret Mead to say, "Never doubt that a small group of
thoughtful, committed citizens can change the world. Indeed, it is the
only thing that ever has." Or for Buckminster Fuller to observe that "by

changing the minds of 5 percent of the population, one could effectively change the way society operates."[1] But how does one go about changing the minds of that small, committed 5 percent?

The answer may lie in "the zone of overlap between virtue and self-interest" (in the words of author Stephen Young) and in creating incentives for leaders to pursue "self-interest considered upon the whole."[2]

A practical way to make leaders behave like better stewards is to make it economically and financially worthwhile for them to do so. These leaders include directors and CEOs and CFOs and COOs and CAOs and chairmen and managing directors and partners of financial institutions. The best vehicle we have for doing that may be a new trend, primarily taking hold within the institutional investor community. The trend is to screen for and invest in organizations that demonstrate the ability to manage across environmental, social, and governance issues.

Environmental, social, and governance investing (ESG, for short) is the latest evolution of what is generally referred to as socially responsible investing (SRI). The first examples of SRI in the United States date back to the eighteenth century, when Quakers reputedly refused to invest in weapons and slavery, and to the Revolutionary War, when pacifists boycotted bonds being issued by the Continental Congress because proceeds might end up funding the war.

A practical way to make leaders behave like better stewards is to make it economically and financially worthwhile for them to do so.

Initially, SRI was about negative or exclusionary screening (usually around "sin sectors"): Don't invest in companies that make cigarettes, exploit child labor, distribute alcoholic beverages, operate gambling casinos, or manufacture land mines.

Then, in the 1960s, investors began to leverage ownership rights to influence corporate boards and management. John Harrington, of Harrington Investments, chronicles some of these early shareholder activism campaigns in his book, *Investing with Your Conscience: How to Achieve High Returns Using Socially Responsible Investing*.[3] Table 8.1 highlights some of the milestones since 1995 in ESG investing.

Table 8.1   ESG's Road to Mainstream Acceptance

Milestones in ESG, SRI, and Sustainability Investing

1995	In the U.K., a clause in the Pension Act of 1995 required pension fund executives to disclose how they consider ESG issues in the investment process. Similar regulations were subsequently introduced throughout Europe and pushed demand for investment strategies that integrate ESG factors in the region.
1998	A letter issued by the U.S. Department of Labor states that socially responsible funds meet the fiduciary standards of the Employee Retirement Income Security Act (ERISA).
2000	First regulation introduced in the U.K. establishing that ESG considerations are legal within the fiduciary framework for pension fund trustees. Broader implications for Europe helped to drive ESG investing forward on the Continent.
2003	The U.S. Securities and Exchange Commission adopted amendments to require managers of mutual funds to disclose relevant information about their proxy voting practices.
2005	The United Nations' Principles for Responsible Investment launched. During the same year, a separate study by the UN Environment Program and London-based law firm Freshfields Bruckhaus Deringer LLP went further to say that ESG is not only legal, but an essential part of the fiduciary duties of pension fund trustees.
2010	Establishment of the U.K. Stewardship Code, which sets out best practices for institutional investors to be responsible shareholders. The code encourages investors to explain the extent to which they have complied with the code, or explain why they haven't. Similar policies are being considered in the Netherlands and the European Union. Separately, the SEC published guidance on climate risk disclosure in SEC filings.

Source: Thao Hua, "ESG's Road to Mainstream Acceptance," *Pensions & Investments,* January 24, 2011; 1998 data by Domini Social Investments, LLC, www.domini.com/common/pdf/DOL-Letter.pdf.

SRI = ESG = Sustainability

One particular example from John Harrington's book includes a case in which a black activist organization called FIGHT (Freedom, Integration, God, Honor, Today) took on the Eastman Kodak Company and the company's hiring practices, which FIGHT believed to be discriminatory. When Eastman Kodak failed to follow through on a commitment to create 600 jobs in Rochester, New York, FIGHT took their case to the company's 1967 shareholders' meeting. With the help of representatives from the United Church of Christ and Unitarian Universalists, who were present at the meeting, they succeeded in pressuring the company to deliver on their hiring promises . . . and to throw in a job-training program for good measure.

A better-known example of investors using their investment dollars to bring about social, political, and economic change took the form of divestment campaigns during the apartheid era in South Africa. Investors fled or threatened to flee from companies who profited from doing business in South Africa.

Another version of SRI—impact investing, also known as community investing—is emerging today as a distinctive asset class, according to a 2010 report from J.P. Morgan. Impact investing involves directing capital to communities underserved by traditional financial services. Microfinance is probably the most widely known form of impact investing. Another focus of practitioners of impact investing is companies that offer innovative solutions to challenges like water scarcity or renewable energy. Many foundations have also found ways to create concentrated impacts through mission-related investing, through which foundations seek to align their investments with the focus of their grant making.

Today, impact investing and mission-related investing are among the many variants and versions of SRI, including responsible investing, ethical investing, and values-based investing. These approaches are powered by many different investment philosophies and methodologies, including: engagement (leveraging ownership rights to influence corporate boards and management), negative screening (avoiding sin sectors as previously described), thematic investing (focusing on companies that offer innovative solutions to challenges like water scarcity or renewable energy), and community investing (directing capital to communities underserved by traditional financial services).

Practitioners of these approaches include institutional asset managers like mutual funds, sovereign wealth funds, foundations and endowments, pension funds, and, increasingly, high net worth individuals who work with investment advisors.

The most recent innovation in socially responsible investing is ESG investing—also known as sustainable investing. As we see later in the chapter, ESG represents a fundamental shift from largely moral considerations as the primary basis for investment decisions, to an emphasis on economic best practices and sustainable operating practices. ESG investing is about examining the corporate responsibility practices of corporations for indications of how companies, and those companies' stock prices, will perform over long time periods.

Currently, practitioners of socially responsible investing are involved in a sort of war of journal articles as to what the most effective SRI approach is for generating superior investment returns, influencing the behavior of corporate leaders and effecting societal change. As the Social Investment Forum Foundation puts it:

> What unites these diverse investment approaches—and what ultimately distinguishes them from the broader universe of assets under management . . . is precisely the explicit incorporation of ESG issues into investment decision-making, fund management or shareholder activities. The specific ESG factors and the way they are used may differ widely from investor to investor, and tactical and technical considerations are often specific to an institution or fund manager. But the basic strategies . . . share sufficient features to be observed and measured.[4]

Amy Domini, founder of Domini Social Investments and author of *Socially Responsible Investing: Making Money While Making a Difference,* puts it clearly and simply: "What makes a manager a specialist in socially responsible investing? . . . [T]hey select investments by applying standards that include impacts on people and the planet."[5]

Pax World Investments president and CEO Joseph Keefe offers a similarly succinct definition of the ESG incarnation of socially responsible investing: "the full integration of environmental, social, and governance (ESG) factors into investment analysis and decision making . . . premised on the financial *materiality* of [those] ESG factors."[6]

Environmental, Social, and Governance Issues: Some Examples of Issues that Socially Responsible Investors Are Concerned About[7]

Environmental Issues
- Climate change
- Water scarcity

- Local environmental pollution and waste management
- New regulations expanding the boundaries of environmental product liability

Social Issues
- Workplace health and safety
- Labor and human rights issues
- Government and community relations
- Charitable giving
- Workforce diversity

Governance Issues
- Board structure and accountability
- Accounting and disclosure practices, transparency
- Executive compensation
- Management of corruption and bribery issues
- Money laundering and terrorist financing

The idea behind ESG investing is that companies that engage in sustainable business practices will, on average, perform better over time. These business practices include minimizing their carbon footprint, minimizing their consumption of scarce resources or degradation of the environment, treating their employees well, and not only recognizing but celebrating diversity in their workforces. ESG companies have put in place responsible governance practices around compensation and give back to and invest in the communities in which their employees, customers, and clients live and work. Table 8.2 shows companies that are considered attractive ESG investments, and why.

What underlies the hypothesis that ESG-leading companies will outperform their competitors over time?

For one thing, ESG investors believe, the business practices described here are indicators of the quality of management.

Writes Goldman Sachs, "ESG performance [is] a proxy for management quality, in so far as it reflects the company's ability to respond to long-term trends and maintain a competitive advantage."[8]

ESG investors also believe the kinds of enlightened business practices described here can serve to reduce risk, whether it be litigation risk, the risk of running out of inputs like water and energy, regulatory risk, or reputational risk.

Table 8.2   Striving to Meet a Higher Standard: Six Examples of Companies that Are Considered Attractive ESG Investments

---

Unilever (London, U.K.)

Global food and consumer goods company, whose brands include Lipton, Hellman's, Ben & Jerry's, Dove, Vaseline.

Working to source all its paper and packaging material from recycled or sustainably managed forests by 2020.

Globally more than 20 percent of its tea is sourced from Rainforest Alliance Certified farms.

Committed to sourcing 100 percent of its fish from sustainable sources.

Novo Nordisk A/S (Bagsvaard, Denmark)

Danish pharmaceutical company focused on the discovery, development, manufacturing, and marketing of diabetes-management products.

Access to Medicines program supplies insulin to 36 of the poorest countries, including Cameroon and Tanzania.

Established 13 clinics and enrolled about 800 diabetic children in the Changing Diabetes in Children program.

Sold insulin to 33 countries at or below a price of 20 percent of the average prices for insulin in the Western world.

Johnson Controls (Milwaukee, Wisconsin, United States)

Automotive systems manufacturer. A leading supplier of lithium-ion batteries for hybrid vehicles.

A signatory of the UN Global Compact and Caring for Climate, a global effort by the UN Global Compact and World Business Council for Sustainable Development.

Pledged to work with Clinton Climate Initiative (CCI) and city governments to improve energy efficiency.

Developed www.MakeYourBuildingsWork.com for building owners to estimate the energy and operational cost savings and carbon emission reductions that can be achieved.

Deere & Company (Moline, Illinois, United States)

Founded in 1837, Deere & Company is in the agricultural, construction, turf and forestry equipment markets.

John Deere EHS Management System includes documented processes for controlling and continuously improving environmental stewardship measures.

(Continued)

Table 8.2 *Continued*

Third party audits are conducted at all manufacturing sites to verify compliance with the standard.

Uses recycled or renewable materials in some of its products, such as corn- and soy-based plastics for some components.

Southwest Airlines Company (Dallas, Texas, United States)
The largest U.S. domestic air carrier.

Southwest's pay and benefits are above the industry average.

The first airline to establish profit sharing. Employees currently own 5 percent of company stock.

Cultivates a culture of "employees first" with the idea that it will lead to customer satisfaction and profits at the airline, which has been profitable for 38 consecutive years.

Participates in the Air Transport Association of America's initiative to voluntarily reduce GHG emissions by 30 percent between 2005 and 2025.

Becton, Dickinson and Company (Franklin Lakes, New Jersey, United States)
A global medical technology company that develops, manufactures, and sells medical devices, instrument systems, and reagents, including for infectious diseases and cancers.

Partners with the International Council of Nurses to establish wellness centers for healthcare workers in Africa.

Uses low-tech methods to prevent seven types of waste: inefficient processing, unnecessary motions, waiting, making too much, fixing defects, moving things, and excess inventory.

Executive compensation structure is linked to performance, maintaining a high degree of alignment between pay and the long-term value and financial soundness of the company.

SOURCE: SRI Wealth Management Group, RBC Wealth Management-U.S. Specific company-related ESG research provided by MSCI, Inc. as well as 10-K filings and company sustainability and annual reports.

As the organization Business for Social Responsibility puts it: Many investors see in "strong ESG performance a proxy for strong and effective management. Identification and oversight of ESG issues indicates management that has a high awareness of the company's external operating environment" and "can serve as an indicator for companies' ability to manage risk and adapt in the face of new challenges to their business models."[9]

ESG investing was given a major boost by the publication in 2006 of *Principles for Responsible Investment*. The principles were the work product of a process put into motion in 2005 by the office of the United Nations Secretary General, which convened a group of 20 or so of the world's largest institutional investors. As of September 2011, 900 of the most respected pension funds and investment managers from 47 countries have signed on to the principles[10] (see Figure 8.1), which begin with the following declaration:

> As institutional investors, we have a duty to act in the long-term interest of our beneficiaries. In this fiduciary role, we believe that the environmental, social and governance (ESG) issues can affect the performance of investment portfolios.[11]

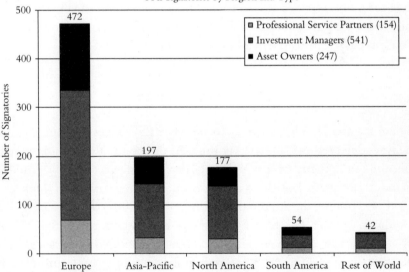

Figure 8.1 Sustainable Investing: Europe Leads the World
SOURCE: Principles for Responsible Investment, www.unpri.org. Data as of November 1, 2011.

The UN principles call for investors to, among other things:

- Incorporate ESG issues into investment analysis and decision-making processes.
- Seek appropriate disclosure on ESG issues by the entities in which [they] invest.[12]

Another catalyst for ESG investing was the financial crisis itself, which exposed the risks of weak corporate governance practices around things like risk management processes and compensation policies.

Institutional Investor suggests that, as a result of the crisis, "Public pension funds, sovereign wealth funds and insurance companies realized that although they had long-term horizons, many of the investment decisions they were making, and the decisions being made by the companies in which they had invested, were short term and in some cases highly risky. The behavior of the major financial institutions—their risk-taking and bonus making in particular—struck some nerves."[13]

"The financial crisis showed investors we weren't monitoring the things that really mattered," says Anne Simpson, senior portfolio manager for global equities at CalPERS. "If you looked on the boards of the big banks, they checked all of the boxes for good corporate governance. But the crisis told us our reading is superficial."[14]

Delivering Alpha

There is considerable debate as to whether ESG investing can actually deliver added returns (alpha) over time. At this point, it's too early to tell, since the time frame over which ESG investing needs to be measured is decades, not years. But there are some encouraging early data points.

For example, during the time from 2005 to 2007, the companies on Goldman Sachs's GS SUSTAIN focus list outperformed the MSCI World Index by 25 percent.[15] While acknowledging that "clearly we do not yet have a long track record of performance in terms of our methodology," Goldman went on to say, "we believe that the early signs are encouraging."[16]

"Incorporating our proprietary ESG framework into the long-term industrial analysis and returns-based analysis of the sectors covered to date . . . has enabled us to select top picks," 72 percent of whom had outperformed their peers, Goldman reported.[17]

A *Pensions and Investments* article cites the research of State Street Global Advisors, suggesting that "there is some preliminary evidence that companies with better ESG ratings offered some downside protection during the financial crisis."[18] Chris McKnett, co-author of the paper, *Sustainable Investing: Positioning for Long-Term Success*, told *P&I* "These companies offered more stability during the worst period of the bear market."[19]

McKnett's paper continues, "Ultimately, it comes down to the basic premise that well-governed companies are likely to be less risky over time. Incorporating an ESG framework may serve as an effective way to protect shareholder value."[20]

Then there is the Domini Social Index (DSI), currently known as the MSCI KLD 400 Social Index. Beginning in 1990, Amy Domini and her partners designed an index that used the S&P 500 as its benchmark, but which screened out companies that were considered underperformers from an environmental, social, and governance perspective. They also added companies that were considered proactive and industry leaders in their approach to incorporating ESG considerations in their business models. Though ESG is an abbreviation that did not exist in 1990 when the index went live, they did screen the portfolios for environment, social, and corporate culture, which included governance issues. The Domini Social Index has outperformed its S&P 500 benchmark on an actual and risk-adjusted basis over 20 years.

What isn't subject to debate is that interest in ESG investing has grown dramatically in recent years, as has assets under management.

"ESG investing has moved to the mainstream of institutional investing from the fringes," trumpets a January 2011 special report by *Pension & Investments*.[21]

ESG assets in the United States grew to more than $3 trillion at the start of 2010, up 380 percent from $639 billion in 1995, the year the Social Investment Forum Foundation started tracking this trend. In the three-year period from 2007 to 2009, during which the S&P 500 declined and conventional investment assets grew by less than 1 percent, SRI assets increased by 13 percent. Today, the Foundation estimates one in eight dollars under professional management in the United States "is involved in some strategy of socially responsible investing."[22] And in Europe—the leader in SRI—SRI assets under management grew even more robustly, up 85 percent in the two-year period from 2008 and 2009 to the equivalent of $6.5 trillion.

In a sign of the increasing importance of ESG investors, a growing number of publicly traded corporations are publicly disclosing data on their ESG performance. State Street Global Advisor research says that according to the Global Reporting Initiative, 1,350 companies from 65 countries issued such reports in 2009.[23] "Puma, a sports footwear and apparel brand that is a subsidiary of the French PPR Group (which also includes Gucci, Stella McCartney, and Yves Saint Laurent) announced . . . that it would begin issuing an environmental profit and loss statement that will account for the full economic impact of the brand on its ecosystem."[24]

As far back as 2007, RBC established a new approach to corporate responsibility. RBC is one of North America's largest financial services companies and has been long recognized as one of the world's most sustainable investment–oriented companies.

The push toward a more systematic approach to sustainability began when RBC was faced with an increasing number of research requests and demands from stakeholders across a diverse set of issues. RBC conducted a full assessment of its global business strategy, mapped out stakeholder interests and concerns, and then identified the points of strongest intersection between its business strategy and stakeholders' interests. For example, banks like RBC are also expected to take responsibility, in some measure, for the actions of their clients, especially those to whom they provide credit.

RBC developed an overall framework, vision, and direction for managing the different elements of corporate responsibility. Dubbed "The RBC Blueprint for Doing Better," RBC's approach is described each year in a 100-page Corporate Responsibility Report. It is outlined in summary form in Figure 8.2.

"It is clear that we have entered an era in which more people are devoting more thought to their investment choices and more scrutiny to the behavior of companies," says the CEO of RBC, Gordon Nixon. "There is no going back, and corporate officers ignore this reality at their peril. It is true that the precise contours of responsibility may be impossible to define for society at large—but more people will be

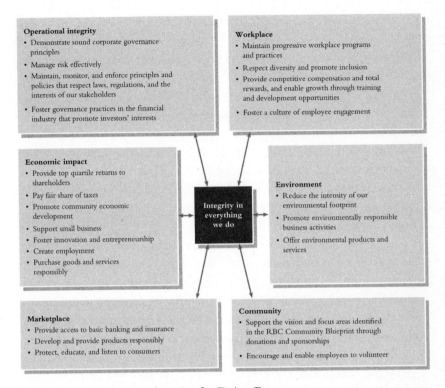

Operational integrity
- Demonstrate sound corporate governance principles
- Manage risk effectively
- Maintain, monitor, and enforce principles and policies that respect laws, regulations, and the interests of our stakeholders
- Foster governance practices in the financial industry that promote investors' interests

Workplace
- Maintain progressive workplace programs and practices
- Respect diversity and promote inclusion
- Provide competitive compensation and total rewards, and enable growth through training and development opportunities
- Foster a culture of employee engagement

Economic impact
- Provide top quartile returns to shareholders
- Pay fair share of taxes
- Promote community economic development
- Support small business
- Foster innovation and entrepreneurship
- Create employment
- Purchase goods and services responsibly

Integrity in everything we do

Environment
- Reduce the intensity of our environmental footprint
- Promote environmentally responsible business activities
- Offer environmental products and services

Marketplace
- Provide access to basic banking and insurance
- Develop and provide products responsibly
- Protect, educate, and listen to consumers

Community
- Support the vision and focus areas identified in the RBC Community Blueprint through donations and sponsorships
- Encourage and enable employees to volunteer

Figure 8.2   The RBC Blueprint for Doing Better
SOURCE: Royal Bank of Canada, 2010 Corporate Responsibility Report and Public Accountability Statement, 8.

defining these contours for themselves. They'll be deciding for themselves what constitutes a responsible company. And they will be investing their money accordingly."[25]

Virtually the entire November 2011 edition of the *Harvard Business Review* was dedicated to multiple articles on the topic "How Great Companies Think Differently." Inside excerpts from the magazine read: "The companies that perform best over time build a social purpose into their operations that is as important as their economic purpose," and "Instead of being mere money-generating machines, they combine financial and social logic to build enduring success."[26]

In 2008, Mercer, a leading investment consultant, announced it would incorporate ESG questions and analysis into its investment manager searches.[27]

In a 2009 survey of global investment managers, 63 percent of the respondents said they were in the process of including ESG undertakings into contracts with investment managers—up from 38 percent the year before.[28]

Fidelity Investments now offers ESG information to its investors as a part of its online investing tools.[29]

A Virtuous Cycle

The more assets under management in ESG and other SRI strategies, the more potential dollars are available to flow, at the margin, to the stocks of companies that rank high on ESG scales. And the more demand for those stocks, the better the potential total shareholder return performance of highly ranked companies.

The result? "Companies with strong ESG performance are presumably rewarded for their investments in corporate responsibility programs through improved analyst ratings, more investor interest, and potentially a higher stock price."[30] Or to put it slightly differently, "investors increasingly seek out companies with positive environmental, social and governance performance not because they are morally admirable but because they are more viable in the long run."[31]

Explains Tom Van Dyck, founder of and principal at RBC's SRI Wealth Management Group in San Francisco: "A management team that embraces the idea of sustainability—uses it to lower their costs, increase their revenues, improve their brand, reduce their risk, and attract talented people—will outperform you, if they are your competitors. That outperformance increases the weighted average cost of capital for companies that have 'bad' practices from an ESG perspective, and decreases the cost for those that have better ESG practices."[32]

> "A management team that embraces the idea of sustainability . . . will outperform you."
> —Tom Van Dyck, SRI Wealth Management Group

Vinay Nair, an adjunct professor at Columbia Business School, told *Institutional Investor* that "if an additional 5 percent of the total capital is allocated to sustainability in the equity markets over the next three years, companies that are recognized as 'good' will outperform 'bad' ones by 3 percentage points annually."[33]

In a world in which a substantial percentage of executive compensation is linked to absolute or relative share price performance, this is where the incentive for responsible Stewardship is to be found.

In a seminal 2010 speech to the Boston Economic Club, Joseph Keefe, president and CEO of Pax World Investments, envisioned, "A sort of virtuous cycle would be created: investors rewarding stock prices where sustainability is integrated, and companies responding by further improving their sustainability performance."[34]

"[T]his isn't just about harvesting superior returns," Keefe said, "It's also about affecting corporate behavior and ultimately market behavior."[35]

It may be that ESG investors can affect equity valuations of corporations that rank highly along the dimensions of Stewardship excellence. If so, we will have found all the leverage we need to reward leaders who act like responsible stewards, and change the behaviors of those who don't.

This is the enormous potential of ESG investing.

It's already happening. A 2011 survey of 3,203 executives by McKinsey & Company found that "many companies are actively integrating sustainability principles into their businesses . . . and they are doing so by pursuing goals that go far beyond earlier concern for reputation management—for example, saving energy, developing green products, and retaining and motivating employees, all of which help companies capture value through growth and return on capital."[36]

In an interview with Charlie Rose at the Securities Industry and Financial Markets Association annual meeting in November 2011, Citigroup CEO Vikram Pandit introduced the concept of "responsible finance." He told the group: "At Citi . . . I tell my people you better ask yourself three questions before you do anything or enter into any transaction with a client. [One:] Is it in our clients' interests? Two: Does it add any economic value to anybody? And three: Is it systemically responsible? Those are the three questions and the answer to those three questions has to be yes. Then you are practicing responsible financing."[37]

> *"The long-sought alignment of a firm's prosperity with the best interests of the planet seems not only possible but inevitable."*
>
> —Harvard Business Review

As authors Yvon Chouinard, Jib Ellison, and Rick Ridgeway write in the *Harvard Business Review*, "Progress in each area spurs progress in the others, to the extent that the long-sought alignment of a firm's prosperity with the best interests of the planet seems not only possible but inevitable."[38]

Part of that potential is the possibility that ESG investing could also strengthen financial markets. As a report by the World Bank's International Finance Corporation titled *Future Proof?* ambitiously puts it: "Increased consideration of environmental, social, and governance issues will ultimately lead to better investment decisions, create stronger and more resilient financial markets, and contribute to the sustainable development of societies."[39]

"There can be no better way to restore public confidence in the markets and build a prosperous economic future."[40]

Interlude
It's a Long Life:
The Trouble with Short-Termism

My father, a nuclear physicist at Yale University, came home every evening from his office in Gibbs Laboratory, or from teaching in a classroom, and sat down to drink a martini while reading the newspaper. He tuned out the din of his three sons, enjoyed a glass of wine with my mother at dinner, and then headed back to the lab or his study to put in a final couple of hours of work on whatever bubble-chamber experiment he was focused on at the time. (Mind you, this was a man who named the family dog after an atomic particle, Meson, and whose gift to his first grandchild was a T-shirt from the Fermilab particle accelerator facility in Illinois.)

I remember asking him one evening during a visit home why he always drank at dinner if he was planning to go back to work.

He sighed, put down his paper and looked at me over his glasses and said, slowly, "It's a long life."

How well, today, I know what my father meant. It is, indeed, a long life.

The horizons over which Stewardship effectiveness must necessarily be measured are generally decades or generations.

By contrast, the time horizons on which financial services firms and employees are measured today are relatively short. They are tied to financial performance and reporting cycles, namely months or quarters or years.

"The more fundamental problem," writes Steven Pearlstein in the *Washington Post*, ". . . is that the components of modern finance—the securities, the trading and investment strategies, the financing techniques, the technology, the fee structures and the culture in which they operate—are all designed to . . . maximize short-term results."[41]

This has "robbed the economy of the patient capital it needs to produce sustained and vigorous economic growth," Pearlstein wrote.

(Continued)

A 2009 report by the Aspen Institute titled "Overcoming Short-Termism" confirmed this dynamic and found it to be a systemic issue. The very structure of the corporate and financial world is one big web of relationships of people who are enriched by short-term gains, "with contributions by and interdependency among corporate managers, boards, investment advisers, providers of capital and government."[42]

The report concluded that "properly incentivized institutions of different kinds can contribute to long-term wealth creation." Yet fund managers' "primary focus on short-term trading gains" and short-term institutional investors' focus on "quarterly earnings and other short-term metrics" works to "harm the interests of shareholders seeking long-term growth and sustainable earnings."[43]

A parallel form of short-termism can infect individual investors. James Montier, a member of GMO's asset allocation team, recalling Warren Buffett's analogy of "waiting for the fat pitch," describes it this way:

"[M]ost investors seem unable to wait, forcing themselves into action at every available opportunity, swinging at every pitch, as it were. As tempting as it may be to be a 'man of action,' it often makes more sense to act only at extremes. But the discipline required to 'do nothing' for long periods of time is not often seen."[44]

Patient capital, the key to long-term value creation, both requires and rewards the long-term orientation that Stewardship is all about. As my father said, it's a long life.

Chapter 9

Communities, Caring, and Commitment

Reconnecting with Our Stewardship Responsibilities

Greed doesn't cut it as a satisfying explanation for the current financial crisis. Greed was necessary but insufficient. . . . The fixable problem isn't the greed of the few but the misaligned interests of the many.

— Michael Lewis and David Einhorn

The financial crisis gave us a preview of what happens when we lose touch with our Stewardship responsibilities. We have seen the ending to a movie that might have been titled *Losing Our Way*—at least as it played out in the financial sector of G-20 developed nations in 2008 and 2009.

But precisely the same thing is happening today in other sectors. And the consequences will be just as devastating—not only financially, but to the fabric of society and our quality of life in the United States and throughout the world—if we don't step up to find a way to reconnect with and reestablish a Stewardship ethic in all human undertakings.

In too many areas, we see a focus on short-term gratification at the expense of long-term Stewardship. We see leaders ducking accountability for fixing critical, but seemingly intractable, problems. We see a lack of integrity, humility, purposefulness—in other words, a deficit in all of the characteristics of responsible Stewardship. "The financial crisis is . . . akin to the sustainability crisis, in that it was set in motion by a species of short-term thinking not unrelated to the short-term thinking that is undermining our planet's ecological balance," says Joseph F. Keefe, president and CEO of Pax World Management.[1]

Fiscal Stewardship

The most recent examples of this involve the sovereign creditworthiness of the United States and of European nations like Ireland, Greece, Spain, Portugal—even Italy and France. Unsustainable entitlement programs—promises made by governments over many decades to their constituents—threaten to tip economies weakened by the financial crisis into painful debt spirals.

Incredibly, the world watched in the summer of 2011 what the *Wall Street Journal* called "the road to fiscal perdition":[2] the spectacle of the U.S. Congress holding the creditworthiness of the U.S. government hostage. The issue is how to restore the nation's public finances to some form of balance when (a) the present value of future outlays under entitlement spending programs (principally Social Security, Medicare, and Medicaid) was $46 trillion as of 2009, according to the Congressional Budget Office, almost four times the outstanding balance of U.S. Treasury debt;[3] and (b) those three programs—which currently constitute 40 percent of federal spending and which, together with interest on the national debt, equals 70 percent of revenues—are growing faster than the economy and faster than revenues.[4] (See Figure 9.1.)

Neither Republicans nor Democrats were willing to acknowledge what was and is plainly obvious to most observers: namely, that reducing the deficit and reducing our debt-to-GDP ratio will require a combination

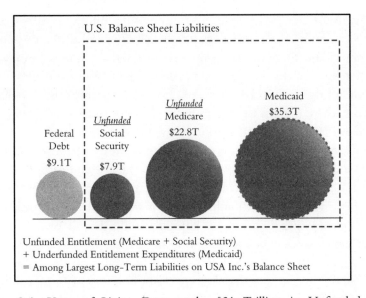

U.S. Balance Sheet Liabilities

Medicaid
$35.3T

Unfunded
Medicare
$22.8T

Unfunded
Social
Security

Federal
Debt

$9.1T

$7.9T

Unfunded Entitlement (Medicare + Social Security)
+ Underfunded Entitlement Expenditures (Medicaid)
= Among Largest Long-Term Liabilities on USA Inc.'s Balance Sheet

Figure 9.1 Years of Living Dangerously: $31 Trillion in Unfunded U.S. Commitments are Three Times Bigger than U.S. Debt
SOURCE: Mary Meeker, "A Basic Summary of America's Financial Statements," USA Inc., ix.

of entitlement cuts, revenue increases, and a growing economy. Of course, the problem is, entitlement cuts are a nonstarter for the Democrats, and revenue increases are a nonstarter for Republicans. While a shotgun eleventh-hour compromise averted default, at least until the next budget deadline, none of the core issues driving what the Committee on the Fiscal Future of the United States in 2010 testimony before the Senate Budget Committee described as "the unsustainability of today's budget problems" have been addressed. Without changes to the federal budget, debt as a percentage of GDP will surpass 100 percent in the late 2020s and 200 percent in 2040—meaning "the market for [U.S.] debt would collapse long before 2040."[5] This is why the rating agency Standard & Poor's downgraded the credit of the U.S. Treasury from AAA to AA+ for the first time in our nation's history.

"Above all, S&P's verdict is based on the uselessness of America's politicians," *The Economist* reported.[6] "America's governance and policy-making are becoming 'less stable, less effective and less predictable.'"[7]

Quite the indictment of our capacity for effective fiscal Stewardship.

At about the same time, and continuing into the fall of 2011, European bank stocks went into free fall on fears about the credit-worthiness and therefore the valuation of fixed-income securities held on their balance sheets. This time, the fixed-income securities at issue are not mortgage-backed securities, but more perniciously, sovereign debt issued by nations on the periphery of the European Union—the so-called PIIGS: Portugal, Ireland, Italy, Greece, and Spain.

The same concerns about contagion that created panic in 2008 and 2009 emerged again in the fall of 2011. These include fears that the failure of a major European bank could drag other financial institutions into crisis. The way that could happen is that a European bank could have exposure either directly or through credit default swaps, on sovereign debt, or on debt issued by the banks that hold sovereign debt as assets on their balance sheets. This was a possibility made all the more plausible by the fact that the sovereign debt holdings of European banks in 2011 dwarfed their mortgage-backed securities holdings at the height of the crisis of 2008–2009. (See Figure 9.2.) Indeed, Credit Suisse projects that European bank losses from markdowns and defaults in sovereign debt could eventually exceed the aggregate losses they have incurred to date from subprime mortgage holdings.

Stewardship failures in the form of fiscal mismanagement in the United States constitute a future crisis—Charles Dickens's Ghost of Christmas Future, so to speak. By contrast, in Europe, fiscal mismanagement constitutes a clear and present crisis, the Ghost of Christmas Present.

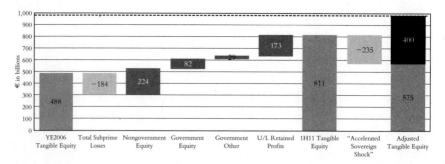

Figure 9.2 European Banks Sovereign Debt Losses Could Dwarf Subprime Losses
SOURCE: "European Banks: The Lost Decade," Credit Suisse Securities Europe, Equity Research, September 15, 2011. (Credit Suisse data and estimates.)

"Fighting for its life," trumpets a headline in *The Economist*. "The euro zone is in intensive care."[8]

"It is an undisputable fact," wrote Germany's finance minister, Wolfgang Schäuble, in the *Financial Times*, "that excessive state spending has led to unsustainable levels of debt and deficits that now threaten our economic welfare."[9]

As Table 9.1 shows, gross debt as a percent of gross domestic product (GDP) ranged in the fall of 2011 from 115 percent in Ireland to 120 percent in Italy to 121 percent in Portugal to 154 percent in Greece. By 2014, those ratios are expected to increase to as high as 147 percent in Ireland, 134 percent in Portugal, and 99 percent in Spain (holders of Greek bonds have already accepted the inevitability of their bonds' default and agreed to partial repayment.) A 100 percent debt-to-GDP ratio is generally considered the point of no return beyond which debt service obligations begin to strangle an economy and push it into a debt spiral, out of which it is no longer possible to grow.

The root cause of the European sovereign debt crisis is not the bubble in housing prices that precipitated the crisis of 2008–2009. Instead, it can be found in decades of the same failure of Stewardship in fiscal policy that the United States has recently started to demonstrate.

Policy makers and politicians have acted like "children at play," investor and commentator Jeremy Grantham told *MarketWatch*. "No one has been prepared to make tough decisions. Where have the Europeans been for 10 years? None of these things came out of the woodwork two weeks ago [in the fall of 2011]. No one attempted to blow the whistle and make tough decisions in a timely fashion."[10]

> *The root cause of the European sovereign debt crisis . . . can be found in decades of the same failure of Stewardship in fiscal policy that the United States has recently started to demonstrate.*

In an article ominously titled, "Be Afraid," *The Economist* points to a "failure of honesty" at the core of the European crisis. "Too many rich-world politicians have failed to tell voters the scale of the problem. . . . At a time of enormous problems, the politicians seem Lilliputian. That's the real reason to be afraid."[11]

Table 9.1 European Countries Drowning In Debt

Comparative European Country Sovereign Debt Burden

(EUR bn)	Austria	France	Germany	Greece	Italy	Portugal	Ireland	Spain	Sweden	UK
Total Government Debt in Issue	191	1282	1240	339	1591	140	90	635	110	1218
10-year+ as % of Total	25	19	13	19	24	12	9	17	12	47
10 > x > 2 as % of Total	63	49	46	45	45	62	73	48	60	36
<2 years as % of Total	13	32	41	20	31	26	18	35	28	17
2011 Budget Deficit/GDP (%)	−3.5	−5.8	−2.1	−8.7	−4.3	−6.5	−11.5	−6.7	0.1	−8.6
Source:	RBC	IMF	RBC	RBC	IMF	RBC	RBC	RBC	IMF	IMF
2011 Gross Govt Debt/GDP (%)	73	85	83	154	120	121	115	64	37	83
2011 Current Account Balance	3.1	−2.8	−5.1	−8.2	−3.4	−8.7	0.2	−4.8	6.1	−2.4
Country 5-year CDS (bp)	66	80	40	1926	175	791	771	289	24	64
Country 10-year CDS (bp)	73	97	60	1609	180	697	682	287	37	81

SOURCE: RBC Capital Markets estimates, IMF, ECB. European Banks: The Euro Periphery Sovereign Crisis and Implications for European Bank Sector, June 20, 2011.

Environmental Stewardship

Then there's the environmental sustainability crisis popularized by former vice president Al Gore and his documentary movie, *An Inconvenient Truth*. The problem is climate change due to greenhouse gas emissions from carbon-intensive energy sources that, if not reduced, could reach a tipping point. The dangers include the melting of polar caps, rising sea levels, deforestation, more volatile weather patterns with attendant risks of natural disasters, including more frequent droughts and more severe floods, and even species extinction.

As *The Economist* notes, "Humans have become a force of nature reshaping the planet on a geological scale—but at a far-faster-than-geological speed." The magazine goes on to state that the role of humans in accelerating these processes is so profound that geologists and other scientists have begun to informally refer to the current period as the "Anthropocene."[12]

We are also facing the twin sustainability crises of population growth coupled with a simultaneous scarcity of critical resources on which human existence depends. At today's rates, the number of people living on the planet will increase from about 7 billion to more than 9 and possibly 10 billion by the year 2050. As demand for everything increases, we are experiencing shortages of oil, metals, potassium, and phosphorus (fertilizer). Clean fresh water, for which there is no alternative, is becoming scarcer. Topsoil is eroding faster than it is being replaced, threatening agricultural production. Already, crop yields per acre have declined from 3.5 percent in the 1960s to 1.2 percent today.[13] Air quality is deteriorating. The capacity of the planet to sustain life is diminishing, even as the number of people living on it is growing at exponential rates.

"How we deal with this unsustainable surge in demand . . . is going to be the greatest challenge facing our species," writes Jeremy Grantham.[14]

Commentators like Thomas Friedman of the *New York Times* have pointed to these developments as evidence of a generational shortcoming on the part of baby boomers. The boomers have taken the inheritance given us by the "Greatest Generation," TV newsman Tom Brokaw's term, and squandered it. "We, alas, in too many ways, have been what the writer [and founder of *Spy* magazine] Kurt Andersen called 'The Grasshopper Generation,' eating through the prosperity that was bequeathed us like hungry locusts," writes Friedman.[15] Future generations are left with the legacy of environmental degradation, crushing public sector debt and entitlement burdens, and a planetary population whose demands could outstrip available resources within the next half century. The culprit is the "frozen-in-the-headlights response we are showing right now in the face of the distant locomotive quite rapidly approaching and . . . whistling loudly."[16]

But it's not too late. All of these are solvable problems. All of these are problems that responsible stewards can and would solve.

Wanted: Responsible Stewards

"We humans have the brains and the means to reach real planetary sustainability," writes Grantham. "The problem is with us and our focus on short-term growth and profits, which is likely to cause suffering on a vast scale. With foresight and thoughtful planning, this [the prospect of human] suffering is completely avoidable."[17]

"The problem is not what we are *capable* of, but of how we will actually behave."[18]

Somewhat ironically, it may ultimately be the financial crisis of 2008–2009 and the ensuing global response to making the financial system safer, sounder, and more secure—the 235 rulemaking mandates in the Dodd-Frank Wall Street Reform and Consumer Protection Act and the capital, leverage, and liquidity rules proposed by the Financial Stability Board and Basel Committee—that demonstrates that we do in fact have the capacity to act like responsible stewards.

"The problem is not what we are capable *of, but of how we will actually behave."*

—Jeremy Grantham

I started this book writing about the leaders of financial institutions, about how the financial crisis was caused, or at least aggravated, by the failure on their part to live up to their Stewardship responsibilities. "The captains of finance and the public stewards of our financial system ignored warnings and failed to question, understand, and manage evolving risks within a system essential to the well-being of the American public," in the words of *The Financial Crisis Inquiry Report*.[19]

To a very great extent, the path forward—to capital markets' stability, to restoring public trust and confidence in the financial system, to minimizing the severity of future financial crises, to economic growth— requires a renewed commitment on the part of financial industry leaders to a twenty-first century version of servant leadership.

> *The path forward—to "fiscal sustainability" and "planetary sustainability"—requires that not just our leaders, but* all of us, *reconnect with our Stewardship responsibilities.*

No amount of legislation, and no amount of regulatory rulemaking, will ultimately be able to overcome or compensate for failures in leadership.

As the poet and French revolutionary, Louis de Saint-Just, once wrote: "Too Many Laws, Too Few Examples."*

"Where have all the leaders gone?" asks Bill George in *Authentic Leadership*.[20]

He continues: "*We need new leadership.* We need authentic leaders, people of the highest integrity, committed to building enduring organizations. We need leaders who have a deep sense of purpose and are true to their core values. We need leaders who have the courage to build their companies to meet the needs of all their stakeholders, and who recognize the importance of their service to society."[21]

But it's not just about leadership. The path forward—to "fiscal sustainability" and "planetary sustainability"—requires that not just our leaders, but *all of us*, reconnect with our Stewardship responsibilities.

Alone in a Dark Room

I asked my lifelong friend and tennis partner, Brian Walsh, what needs to happen to prevent similar crises in the future. I first met Brian on the

---

*After receiving a draft manuscript of my book, RBC's head of Global Wealth Management, George Lewis, saw this inscription carved into the wall of a building at 21 Davies Street while on a business trip to London and sent it to me as a synopsis of what he viewed to be a core premise of this book.

clubhouse porch at the Club de Golf de La Malbaie, on the northern shore of the St. Lawrence River, 90 miles north of Quebec City, when I was 13 years old.

The club was the summer golf course of my great-grandfather, President William Howard Taft.

Brian grew up to become the president of Bankers Trust's Canadian subsidiary and then ran BT's global derivatives business before founding Saguenay Capital, a New York–based hedge fund advisory and fund of funds firm. Walsh is also a respected advisor to one of the wealthiest families in Canada.

He told me: "The only answer is a religious one: what values get celebrated."

"It's a societal problem. Take excesses in the mortgage finance sector. It wasn't just the securitizers—the banks and broker-dealers—that contributed to the problem. It was the mortgage brokers. It was the servicers. It was Fannie Mae and Freddie Mac. It was the rating agencies. It was the borrowers themselves. Everyone was in on it.

"Honestly, what we need is some kind of spiritual revival. We have to change what people value. We've had several generations living out their lives under the working premise that God is dead. Well, if God is dead, there are no absolutes. If there are no absolutes, there is no right or wrong. If there is no right or wrong, then anything goes.

"Until that changes . . . we won't change the fundamental cause of the last financial crisis and we won't prevent future crises from occurring."

In my view, we need to not only fix "the greed of the few." We must also address "the misaligned interests of the many," as Michael Lewis and David Einhorn wrote in the *New York Times*.[22]

The notion that the causes of the serial crises we are facing go beyond mere leadership failure is one Lewis has been exploring recently. In his recently published book, *Boomerang*, in a chapter on the municipal debt crisis in the United States, Lewis describes the bankruptcy of the city of Vallejo, California, in terms of garden-variety plundering: "The people who had power in the society, and were charged with saving it from itself, had instead bled the society to death."[23]

But then Lewis goes on to say, "The problem . . . isn't a public-sector problem; it isn't a problem with government; it's a problem with the entire society. . . . It's a problem of people taking what they can, just because they can, without regard to the larger social consequences."[24]

"Alone in a dark room with a pile of money, Americans knew exactly what they wanted to do, from the top of society to the bottom. They'd been conditioned to grab as much as they could, without thinking about the long-term consequences."[25]

Early in my career, I worked for two years as an aide to the Mayor of Saint Paul, Minnesota—a bearded, lisping Lebanese labor lawyer named George Latimer. I may be the only CEO of a major brokerage firm who has worked in a city hall. The mayor used to joke that he hired me because he felt at least one out of the thousands of public employees working for the city ought to be a Republican.

Part of my job involved writing speeches for the mayor, one of which ended up being a meditation on the nature of community. Community, I wrote, exists to the extent that people feel and recognize and act on the recognition that they have a responsibility to other members of the community.

> *"We are alive not for ourselves but for one another."*
>
> —Henri Nouwen

As Henri Nouwen puts it in *Bread for the Journey*, "[Community] grows from the spiritual knowledge that we are alive not for ourselves but for one another."[26] What differentiates communities that work from those that don't is the degree to which community members feel accountable for and live up to those responsibilities. In other words, what counts is the level of Stewardship ethic that exists in the community.

Commitment to Community

I believe that communities, like the state of Minnesota, encompass and have a responsibility not just to some of their members, but to all of their members.

As this book is being published and distributed, I am deeply involved in efforts to defeat the passage of a proposed amendment to the Minnesota state constitution that will be on the ballot in November 2012. The amendment would hardwire into the state constitution a definition of marriage as a union only between a man and a woman. I am involved because my oldest daughter and my step-daughter are lesbians. I am involved because I am the executive sponsor for RBC's GLBT (Gay, Lesbian, Bisexual, and Transgender) employee resource group. I am involved because I believe that the success of businesses depends on attracting and retaining the best talent in the world and on having a diverse workforce that can understand and respond to the needs of our increasingly diverse client base. I am involved because I believe deeply in the core principle espoused by my grandfather, Robert Alphonso Taft, of equality under the law. But the most important reason I am involved is that I believe a commitment to inclusiveness is the answer to many of the sustainability issues we face today.

The challenge of the path forward is this: We need to move from our historical notions of *community* as small, localized groups of relatively homogenous neighbors, to a vision of larger and more diverse communities . . . to a vision of community at the national level or even at the global level.

"Early humans flourished by expanding their definitions of their 'in group,'" write Doug Lennick and Fred Kiel in *Moral Intelligence 2.0.* "At this time in history, our survival may depend on expanding our 'in group' to include all the people on Earth."[27]

I attended the Taft School, in Watertown, Connecticut, for four years in the late 1960s and early 1970s. Almost every day I walked past a black and white photograph of my grandfather taken in 1953 as he walked across the rotunda of the U.S. Capitol on crutches after his last day on the floor of the U.S. Senate, where he had just transferred his duties as Senate Majority Leader. He was suffering at the time from cancer, diagnosed after a golf outing earlier that year with President Dwight Eisenhower. He died shortly after the photograph was taken.

The Taft School is a college preparatory school founded in 1890 by Horace Taft, the brother of President William Howard Taft (1909–1913). My grandfather graduated from Taft in the Class of 1906. His picture is one in a series of photographs, hanging on the walls of the school's main corridors, of recipients of the Taft School's Citations of Merit. The citations are awarded to alumni who, by demonstrating "something humanitarian apart from vocation" and by "going beyond the ordinary demands of life or occupation," live up to the school's motto, which roughly translates as: "To serve . . . not to be served."

Figure 9.3   Robert A. Taft at the U.S. Capitol
SOURCE: Marvin Koner.

The Taft School motto is a fitting expression of the core principle of Stewardship. The school's Citations of Merit recognize the same "commitment to serve others" that Stewardship is all about.

When I was a student, those words themselves didn't fully resonate with me as they do today, after 30 years of the vocation and demands of the financial services industry. But even then, as now, the photograph of Robert Taft looking into the distance, as if saying goodbye to a lifetime of public service, evokes for me what C. S. Lewis once described as God's ideal—"a man who, having worked all day for the good of posterity . . . , washes his mind of the whole subject, commits the issue to Heaven, and returns at once to the patience or gratitude demanded by the moment that is passing over him."[28]

We are at an inflection point, with sustainability crises on many fronts, including:

- The safety and stability of our financial system and its ability to facilitate economic growth.
- The fiscal soundness of sovereign nations, particularly G-20 nations, in the face of demographic trends and the escalating cost of entitlements.
- The degradation of the environment and the long-term adequacy of planetary resources to sustain life.

In the formulation of Miyamoto Musashi (see Chapter 3), there is an urgent need to both see the effect of today's behaviors on future generations and to act now to prevent potential crises from becoming train wrecks in slow motion.

> *To serve . . . not to be served.*
> —The Taft School

In all cases, the fork in the road on the path forward is between, on the one hand, the path of sustainability and on the other, the path of ruin. The paths are marked and defined by our willingness to embrace and act on our Stewardship responsibilities.

To make our lives about serving others.

To embrace as our mission leaving the world a better place than we found it.

Afterword

Charles D. Ellis

Stewardship is more important to each of us—and to all of us—than we usually realize. The truth is, we crave good stewardship for the world, for our nation, for our state, and for our community, church, schools, neighborhoods, and, most directly, our families.

Just think of our national parks and how grateful we all are that wisdom eclipsed commercial development. Or how much we treasure our cultural and educational institutions and hospitals that have been guided over the years by thoughtful trustees. Every Girl and Boy Scout knows the camper's rule: Leave the woodlands better than you found them. We all know that our universities, thanks to many years of good stewardship, give our children great teaching during their best learning years and the world invaluable new knowledge created through research, because our universities enjoy strong finances developed through good stewardship—a superb gift from generation to generation.

Families blessed with affluence have many reasons to appreciate those sensible ancestors who wisely conserved and increased family assets through prudent investing. Organizations like our great law firms and investment firms can help us be good stewards of our personal and family resources. We expect a lot from them and they have obligations of responsibility to us because they have invited us to give them . . . our trust in stewardship.

Good and faithful stewards, we are taught in Sunday schools and at temple and in mosques, are admired for caring as though they were owners when they were *not* owners. Today's partners in our great law firms, while legally owners of their firms, understand the larger reality that they are *stewards*. The firm was there before them and will continue after them *and* they are responsible to both their predecessors and their successors to be good stewards—to conserve the best attributes from the past and to recruit, train, educate, and select those who will be stewards as partners in the future.

Trust is at the core of stewardship, and all true stewards work at being truly trustworthy: thinking rigorously and independently about complex matters and carefully selecting for the layman the best way forward, not being beguiled by current fashion or bullied by the slings and arrows of economic self-interest, *and* being comfortably accountable for good long-term results.

John Taft and I shared the good fortune to be sons of Yale and so are fortunate beneficiaries of over 300 years of stewardship by Yale trustees whose names we never knew and who never knew either of us. (Of course, John being a Taft, he surely knew a few of Yale's greats.) Yet the concept of stewardship among those brought together in the Yale community—as friends, as proud alumni, as grateful donors, and as admirers of Yale's current leaders—is strong and inspiring.

John and I also share the privilege of careers in investments. We share concern about the disappointing behavior we have seen and we share a deep conviction that "good enough" is *not* good enough in advising investors—not for investors and not for investment managers. We all benefit when wealth and stewardship come together. And we investment professionals are responsible to our profession's traditions and, most particularly, to our clients to be good stewards on three dimensions: our profession, our firms, and our clients' assets.

Appendix A

Balanced Financial Regulation*

I n a book about core principles, it's important we not take for granted why the
financial system needs to be regulated. The need for regulation underlies
Basel III, Dodd-Frank, and other regulatory reforms underway. The following paper by TheCityUK, in conjunction with Oxford Economics, does one
of the best jobs I've seen in outlining the case for, the objectives, and the approach
to responsible financial regulation.

■ ■ ■

The Rationale for Financial Sector Regulation

- Regulation of the financial sector is appropriate to correct for
  identified market imperfections and failures.

*This material is excerpted with permission from "Balancing Growth and Stability in
EU Financial Reform," published by TheCityUK in conjunction with Oxford Economics, on May 24, 2011. The full report is available at www.thecityuk.com/research/
our-work/reports-list/balancing-growth-and-stability-in-eu-financial-reform/.

- But financial regulation also carries a range of costs, for financial firms and for the wider economy, which are important to recognize when framing the regulatory context.

Before considering the scope of regulatory reform, it is useful to review the fundamental rationale for prudential supervision of the financial sector.

The Costs and Benefits of Regulation

The case for regulation of the financial sector depends on the identification of various market imperfections and failures that, in the absence of regulation, would produce suboptimal results that reduce consumer welfare. On this basis, the core goals of financial regulation are essentially threefold:

1. Consumer protection
2. Maintaining the safety and soundness of financial institutions
3. Ensuring systemic stability

As with other sectors of the economy, consumer protection issues in the financial industry can arise when a firm's conduct of business with a consumer is unsatisfactory. *Conduct of business regulation* is designed to establish rules and guidelines about appropriate behavior and business practices in dealing with customers.

The failure of any firm can also harm consumer welfare, and to this extent financial institutions are not unique. But the potential impact on individual consumers can be greater, particularly when a deposit-taking institution fails. As consumers may not be able to judge the safety and soundness of financial firms (due to asymmetric information), this argues for *prudential supervision* to establish appropriate operational standards.

Regulation for systemic reasons may also be warranted because of the externalities associated with the failure of financial institutions. In other words, the wider social and economic costs of failure of financial institutions (particularly banks) may exceed private costs to the owners of the institutions, and such potential wider costs are not incorporated in the decision making of the firm. Also, compared to other sectors of the economy, financial markets are much more inter-dependent, as demonstrated by the very tight interconnections in the interbank market. Events in one financial market or institution may therefore have important consequences for the wider financial system. Moreover, because of the key role of the financial sector in the efficient functioning of modern economies, such disturbances are also likely to have a negative impact on the nonfinancial sector. Public policy inter-vention then is not only a microeconomic question of protecting the welfare of individual savers and investors, but also becomes a macro-economic issue. *Macroprudential regulators* have been tasked with moni-toring and managing these systemic risks.

Against this background, reforms aimed at strengthening the regu-latory architecture to ensure a more robust and better-functioning financial system are to be welcomed. But there is also a risk, as noted by Goodhart et al. (1998),[*] that financial regulation may be wrongly viewed as a free good that imposes no costs upon society. Financial regulation does carry a range of costs, which broadly fall into three categories:

1. The direct costs of paying for the financial regulator(s) itself. Even when these costs are recouped through a direct levy on the financial industry, this is likely to feed through to higher prices for consumers of financial products.
2. The indirect costs of regulation, namely the incremental costs to firms and individuals of activities required by regulators that would not have been undertaken in the absence of regulation. For example, these incremental costs may include some elements of a firm's compliance staff, management time, systems, capital, and liquidity. This burden reduces the efficiency of the financial sector, diluting its potential contribution to the wider economy.
3. The distortion costs arising from the way in which regulation may change the nature, behavior, and competition in markets for financial products. This may have a significant effect on the nature and availability of the products provided by the financial services

---

[*]Goodhart, C., Hartmann, P., Llewellyn, D., Rojas-Suarez, L. & Weisbrod, S. (1998), "Financial Regulation: Why, How and Where Now?", London, Routledge.

industry, which can also negatively affect economic growth and consumer welfare.

Although most countries have relatively good data on the direct costs of the regulatory bodies themselves, there is little data on the much larger secondary costs of financial regulation. Nonetheless, it is important to recognize that these costs exist when framing the regulatory context.

This discussion highlights the existence of a trade-off between tougher prudential regulations that promote financial stability on the one hand and, on the other, giving proper weight to economic growth by allowing well-managed risk taking to support innovation and efficiency in the financial sector. The goal of prudential regulation is to sustain the smooth functioning of the financial intermediation process, not to completely remove risk-taking behavior from the financial system. If financial institutions did not take risks, their social benefits—including the provision of market liquidity, improved risk sharing, and support for financial and economic innovation—would largely disappear. Achieving an appropriate balance is therefore important to ensure that the regulatory regime does not undermine the potential of the financial sector to contribute to wider economic development.

Appendix B

Basel III Regulatory Accord*

A s complicated as the Dodd-Frank Consumer Protection and Wall Street Reform Act was, it doesn't hold a candle to Basel III. The number of regulators involved in Dodd-Frank is dwarfed by the number of regulators involved in Basel reform. While Dodd-Frank focuses on the U.S. financial system, Basel focuses on countries with developed banking systems. Readers of this book may benefit from a more detailed history and road map to the Basel process than was possible in Chapter 5.

■ ■ ■

---

*Background and summary text reprinted with the permission of Oliver Wyman Financial Services. © 2011 Oliver Wyman, Inc. All rights reserved.

Figures and graphs were sourced from, and are published with, the permission of Association for Financial Markets in Europe (AFME).

Background

The 2008–2009 global economic crisis has provided an opportunity for a fundamental restructuring of the approach to risk and regulation in the financial sector. On December 16, 2010, the Basel Committee on Banking Supervision (BCBS) approved a new global regulatory standard to strengthen bank capital adequacy and liquidity, referred to as Basel III. The provisions in the accord are designed to address a number of the risk issues that were revealed by the recent crisis. These provisions aim to improve the quality of the capital banks are required to hold, enhance the coverage of counterparty credit risk, supplement risk-based capital requirements with a gross leverage ratio, and introduce new liquidity standards. The new standards also propose measures to make the capital framework more countercyclical. The proposed Basel III final rules will take effect on January 1, 2013.

The Basel III standards represent an evolution over previous sets of rules formulated by the BCBS in its role as a committee of banking supervisory authorities that provides a forum for regular cooperation on banking supervisory matters, enhances understanding of key supervisory issues and seeks to improve the quality of banking supervision worldwide by framing guidelines and standards in different areas. The BCBS first published a minimum set of capital requirements for banks in 1988. These requirements became known as Basel I (or the 1988 Basel Accord). Basel I primarily focused on credit risk. Bank assets were classified into five categories according to their credit risk, and assigned risk weights of zero (for example home country sovereign debt), 10, 20, 50, and up to 100 percent (this category has, as an example, most corporate debt). Banks with international presence were required to hold capital equal to 8 percent of their risk-weighted assets (RWAs).

In June 2004, the BCBS enhanced the Basel I requirements by publishing a new set of bank capital requirements, as part of an international standard known as Basel II. Basel II uses a "three pillars" framework: (1) minimum capital requirements (addressing risk), (2) supervisory review, and (3) market discipline. Pillar 1 deals with credit risk (calculated using a standardized approach, foundation internal rating-based approach, or advanced internal rating-based approach), market risk (calculated using a Value-at-Risk approach), and operational risk (calculated using the basic indicator approach, the standardized approach, or the internal measurement approach/advanced measurement approach). Pillar 2 aims to facilitate the regulatory review of a bank's capital adequacy by requiring banks to have an adequate assessment process covering all aspects of capital planning and management to ensure [that] an adequate amount of capital is held against all the risks that the bank is exposed to. Pillar 3 aims to complement the minimum capital requirements and supervisory review process by developing a set of disclosure requirements, which will allow the market participants to gauge the capital adequacy of an institution.

In July 2009, the BCBS finalized new rules, often referred to as the Basel II.5 proposals, which mainly aimed to deal with capital requirements for the trading book and securitization positions. The proposals introduce a new incremental risk charge (IRC) for trading book losses due to default and migrations, and a new stressed Value-at-Risk measure to capture the impact of a period of stress on the bank's trading book.

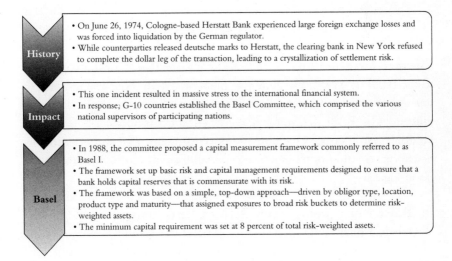

A Brief History of Basel I: The Case of Herstatt
SOURCE: Association for Financial Markets in Europe.

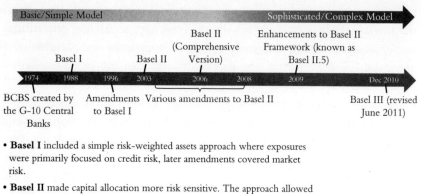

• **Basel I** included a simple risk-weighted assets approach where exposures were primarily focused on credit risk, later amendments covered market risk.

• **Basel II** made capital allocation more risk sensitive. The approach allowed the use of bank's internal models for credit and operational risk.

• Further amendments to Basel II (known as **Basel II.**5) include the revisions to the Basel II market-risk framework and the guidelines for computing capital for incremental risk in the trading book.

• **Basel III** was published in December 2010 and includes significant changes to certain elements of Basel II. These include changes to the quality and quantity of capital and supervisory deductions. It also introduced new liquidity and leverage ratios.

History of Basel Committee on Banking Supervision (BCBS), 1974–2011
SOURCE: Association for Financial Markets in Europe.

Basel III Final Rules Summary

The two consultation documents released by the Basel Committee related to the Basel III standard include five main proposals. Four are designed to strengthen the current regulatory framework by building on the three pillars of the Basel II Capital Accord. The fifth proposal creates a new liquidity framework. This framework aims to introduce internationally harmonized liquidity standards and establish minimum requirements for these standards. These five proposals are summarized next.

1. **Raise the quality, consistency, and transparency of the capital base**

    The proposal attempts to enforce stricter rules governing acceptable forms of capital to ensure [that] banks are in a better position to absorb losses on both a "going concern" and "gone concern" basis.

- Raises the quality of the capital base by mandating that the predominant form of Tier 1 capital must be common shares and retained earnings and by introducing stricter criteria for other elements of Tier 1 capital to ensure that they are sufficiently loss absorbent on a going-concern basis
- Raises the consistency of the capital base by harmonizing the list of regulatory adjustments across Basel Committee countries
- Increases transparency by requiring banks to disclose all elements of capital together with detailed reconciliation to the reported accounts
- Introduces limits (to be calibrated after the impact assessment) for all elements of regulatory capital (i.e., Common Equity, Tier 1 Capital, and Total Capital)

2. Enhance risk coverage

The proposal aims to enforce stricter capital requirements for counterparty credit risk exposures arising from derivatives, repos, and securities financing, and to offer capital incentives to move OTC derivative exposures to central counterparties and exchanges.

- Enhances risk coverage by strengthening the capital requirements and risk management requirements for counterparty credit risk exposures arising from derivatives, repos, and securities financing activities
  - Calculations relying on "worst-case scenario" inputs to determine the specific impact on capital should such a scenario occur
  - Explicit inclusion of wrong-way risk (cases where exposure increases when the credit quality of the counterparty deteriorates) and credit value adjustment (CVA) risk (potential mark-to-market losses associated with the deterioration of the creditworthiness of a counterparty)
  - Capital incentives to use central clearinghouses (zero risk weight in some circumstances)
- Introduces higher capital requirements for lending to financial institutions

3. Supplement risk–based capital requirement with a leverage ratio

The proposal is intended to contain the buildup of leverage by introducing additional safeguards against attempts to arbitrage risk-based requirements, and to reduce model risk and measurement error. However, the precise details of the calculation and calibration of the leverage ratio are still to be determined.

- Introduces a harmonized international minimum leverage ratio to constrain the buildup of gross leverage in the banking sector
- Includes certain off-balance-sheet items in the leverage ratio on the assets side, potentially using a flat 100 percent credit conversion factor

4. Reduce cyclicality and promote countercyclical buffers

The proposal describes a countercyclical framework to encourage the building of capital buffers, but the rules to address procyclicality are still at an early stage of development.

- Reduces the cyclicality of the minimum capital requirements under Pillar 1 by using a "downturn probability of default" measure in the capital calculations
- Promotes stronger provisioning practices (including supporting the initiative of the International Accounting Standards Board to move to an expected loss approach)
- Introduces simple capital conservation rules to ensure that banks build up capital buffers outside periods of stress, which can be drawn down as losses are incurred
- Ensures that the banks' capital requirements take into account the macroeconomic environment in which banks operate

5. Introduce a global liquidity standard

The proposal aims to increase the short-term liquidity coverage and the long-term balance sheet funding by introducing a 30-day liquidity ratio requirement and a one-year structural liquidity ratio. In addition, the proposal lists a common set of monitoring metrics to assist supervisors in identifying and analyzing liquidity risk trends at the bank and system-wide levels.

- Introduces two minimum standards for funding liquidity
  - A 30-day liquidity coverage ratio of high quality liquid assets to total net cash outflows, which is intended to promote short-term resilience to potential liquidity disruptions
  - A one-year structural ratio of available stable funding to required stable funding, which addresses liquidity mismatches,

and provides incentives for banks to use stable sources to fund their activities

6. Outlines a set of standard liquidity monitoring metrics to improve cross-border supervisory consistency

Issues and Solutions from the Recent Financial Crisis: Macroprudential and Market Infrastructure

	Issues	Solutions
Macroprudential	**Impact of financial market cycles propagated through a variety of channels**	• Standards that promote improvements in both capital quality and quantity • Capital buffers (conservation and countercyclical)
	Moral hazard from too big to fail, interconnection between global banks	• Identify the global systemically important banks (G-SIBs) • New assessment methodology proposed by BIS, including the G-SIB buffers
	Ineffective supervision on the macro level	• Revised set of Core Principles • Enhanced country-level reviews through the IMF and World Bank
	Asset price bubbles	• Introduce liquidity and leverage ratios • Develop new macroprudential oversight and enhanced tool kit to detect asset-price bubbles before they get too large
Market Infrastructure	**Inadequate market infrastructure, such as problems in the OTC derivatives market**	• European Market Infrastructure Regulation (EMIR) was proposed by European Commission in September 2010
	Lack of consistent data and the means to carry out proper risk management and surveillance	• Establish legal entity identifier (LEI) standard • Set up key principles for LEI

SOURCE: Association for Financial Markets in Europe.

Issues and Solutions from the Recent Financial Crisis: Microprudential

Issues	Solutions
Insufficient high quality capital available for banks to absorb losses during financial crisis	• A fundamental tightening of the definition of capital • Increase in capital ratio requirements • Significant increase in risk coverage
Liquidity problems—bank liabilities not matched to the duration of their assets during the growth of mortgage products	• Liquidity coverage ratio was introduced • Net stable funding ratio was also introduced by Basel III • Key monitor variables are also required for disclosure such as contractual maturity mismatch on all on- and off-balance-sheet flows
Excessive leverage on banks' balance sheets	• Introduction of leverage ratio based on Tier 1 capital
Allegations of biased ratings from credit rating agencies (CRA), for example, not truly reflecting the risk of a given product	• Stronger oversight regimes for credit rating agencies have been developed
Staff compensation arrangements allegedly drove excessive risk taking	• The FSB principles for sound compensation practices • Pillar 3 disclosure requirements for remuneration
Bank governance is weak and ineffective	• "Principles for enhancing corporate governance" published by BIS

SOURCE: Association for Financial Markets in Europe.

Basel III				
Strengthening Capital	**Enhancing Risk Coverage**	**Leverage**	**Limiting Procyclicality**	**Improving Liquidity Management**
Changes definition of capital to improve quality, consistency and transparency of capital base, increase in the level of core equity and Tier 1 capital, and addition of capital conservation buffer	New standards for counterparty credit risk exposures from derivatives, repos and securities financing transactions	New leverage ratio to constrain buildup of excessive leverage in banking system and provide protection against model risk and measurement error	Introduction of countercyclical buffers in addition to capital requirements that vary with the economic cycle	New liquidity framework which includes two ratios: Liquidity Coverage Ratio and Net Stable Funding Ratio

Basel III Building Blocks

SOURCE: Association for Financial Markets in Europe.

Appendix C

Creating a Clear
Path Forward

I originally wrote this white paper in the fall of 2008 to reassure RBC employees during the heights of the 2008–2009 financial crisis. After I received e-mails from colleagues around the world, this piece went viral and circulated more widely to RBC clients and others. It became a sort of financial crisis equivalent of the memo in the movie Jerry McGuire. It was in writing Creating a Clear Path Forward for clients and employees that I found solid ground.

■ ■ ■

In many ways, we have all been given a once-in-a-lifetime gift.

The financial and economic crisis of the past year has given us the opportunity (in some cases, has forced us) to look into what we were becoming as a society, what we were focusing on as individuals, and to ask ourselves some basic questions about who we are and what is important to us.

I recently met a gentleman who was on US Airways Flight 1549—the plane that made an emergency landing in the Hudson River in January. He heard the engines go quiet and the pilot come on the intercom. He thought what he believed were his last thoughts and he braced for impact. And, when it was all over, he stood out on the wing with the freezing water lapping at his feet, passengers screaming, realizing . . . he had survived.

It occurred to me that his experience is an analogy for what many of us are going through: an emergency landing of our wealth management airplane. The first hint of trouble coming was when Bear Stearns failed. The realization the day Lehman Brothers declared bankruptcy and the Reserve Primary Fund broke the buck that something was, in fact very, very wrong.

The feeling after September 15 and through October and November was that we were in a free fall, about to crash. Then, in December and earlier this year, the hope was that this might, "just" be a down 40 percent emergency landing rather than a total disaster.

Today, we're standing on the airplane's wings. We're shaken, dazed, and confused. We're surrounded by an unbelievable mess. We're still worried about many things—like about fire breaking out, or the plane sinking. Our plans and our schedules are turned upside down and we don't have a clue about how we're going to get to where we were headed just a short time ago.

But we're pretty sure we're going to survive.

Because of what we've just been through and what we are still going through, we've had a glimpse into our tolerance for risk; our real tolerance for risk . . . now that we have had a fresh taste of what life-altering portfolio losses feel like.

We've been given a glimpse into the fragility of the modern financial system and the global economy, which, as it turns out, is more vulnerable than ever expected. This financial system shocks us because of its complexity and interconnectedness.

We've been given a glimpse into the fact that reality is more random than we would like to admit . . . that extreme events really can and do happen. As much as the media, politicians and regulators love to play the "should have, could have" blame game afterwards—and as much as we knew that housing prices were inflated, that risk was underpriced, that financial firms were overly leveraged, and that hedge fund managers were paid unsustainable sums of money—it didn't matter. Black swans cannot be foreseen or predicted.

Most importantly, we were offered a glimpse into our core values and what is truly important to us. We were offered a glimpse into what we'd be left with if everything we've worked for—all our wealth and material possessions—were to go to the ground.

What have we learned and how can we use it going forward? Please allow me to share my own experience. Personally, I've learned that my emotional tolerance for loss is less than my intellectual tolerance for loss. I've learned I need to dial my asset allocation down a notch or two on the model portfolio scale. I've learned that peace of mind, particularly during periods like this, is worth a whole lot of foregone future returns.

I've learned that I was worrying about the wrong things in my investment portfolio. I spent a lot of time focusing on tactical tweaks—like whether to add more large cap exposure (vs. small cap) or more value exposure (vs. growth)—instead of basic, fundamental wealth preservation concerns like: Do I have enough liquidity to make it through a crisis like this? I mean, literally, do I have a way to pay my day-to-day living expenses for a couple of years if the credit markets freeze up and stay frozen?

As Barton Biggs points out in his book *Wealth, War, and Wisdom*, as bad as last year felt, the world has served up periods of social disruption and market volatility way beyond anything we've just experienced—for example, World War II—and probably will again. I bet there are very few people who haven't thought in recent months about what they will do in the future to prepare for the possibility that, as Biggs puts it, "the Four Horsemen . . . ride again."

I've also learned I have certain core beliefs and convictions about how the financial markets operate—like mean reversion, like the predictability of asset class returns over long periods of time, like the value of diversification, in spite of the media's harping about the failure of modern portfolio theory and about there being "no place to hide."

I keep repeating these beliefs to myself like some kind of wealth management version of the Lord's Prayer. In the process, I'm learning that as long as I act on the basis of those core beliefs, not only am I willing to accept the consequences, to go down with the plane, so to speak, but I actually feel better, more in control, than I do just watching the crisis unfold.

Finally, I am embarrassed to say, I've learned that I was probably worshiping some false gods—including the God of Accumulation. I was reminded the hard way that accumulating wealth is by itself, an empty and unsatisfying pursuit. That the best things in life don't cost money; that true wealth lies in relationships. I've learned that the best way to make it through a crisis is to stop focusing on your own problems and to start helping others with theirs.

So I guess insights such as these are the silver lining extreme experiences sometimes offer. The financial crisis of 2008–2009 has enabled us to reconnect with these kinds of core values. Over the past year, we've learned some fundamental lessons about ourselves and about what's truly important to us. And we've been given a tremendous opportunity to act on the basis of what we've learned.

I've chosen to seize this moment for what it is: an appropriate time to begin creating a clear path forward. Based on what I've learned about myself, I'm doing a few things differently. And I'm doing many things the same. But most importantly of all, I'm taking action with a heightened sense of awareness—both of myself and the world around me.

That's the gift the guy standing on the wing of US Airways Flight 1549 was given.

That's the gift we've all been given. What we do now, as individuals, will determine what kind of life we lead today, what kind of choices we'll enjoy making tomorrow and what kind of legacy we leave to our children and grandchildren.

Notes

Introduction

1. John F. Kennedy, *Profiles in Courage* (New York: Harper and Brothers, 1955, 1956), 193.
2. Ibid., 195.

Chapter 1   Core Principles: The Ground Beneath Our Feet

1. Michael Ignatieff, "Getting Iraq Wrong," *New York Times Magazine*, August 5, 2007, 29.
2. Ibid., 28.
3. Sheryl Gay Stolberg, "For Romney, a Role of Faith and Authority," *New York Times*, October 15, 2011.
4. John Cassidy, "Anatomy of a Meltdown: Ben Bernanke, the Fed, and the Financial Crisis," *New Yorker*, December 1, 2008.

Chapter 2   Finance Run Amok: Selfishness Trumps Stewardship

1. Firth Calhoun, "Phil Angelides's Contentious Crew," *Institutional Investor*, February 28, 2011.
2. Steve Forbes, "Transcript: Jeremy Grantham," Forbes.com, January 26, 2009, www.forbes.com/2009/01/23/intelligent-investing-grantham-transcriptJan26.html.

3. Jeremy Grantham, "Night of the Living Fed," quarterly newsletter published by GMO (October 2010).

4. *The Economist*, "Link by Link: The Crash Has Been Blamed on Cheap Money, Asian Savings and Greedy Bankers. For Many People, Deregulation Is the Prime Suspect," October 16, 2008.

5. Peter S. Goodman, "Thieves' Paradise," *New York Times Book Review*, December 26, 2010, 21.

6. Al Watts, *Navigating Integrity* (Minneapolis: Brio Press, 2011), vi.

7. Roger Lowenstein, *The End of Wall Street* (New York: Penguin Press, 2010), 297.

8. Jeremy Grantham, "What a Decade!" quarterly newsletter published by GMO (January 2010), Appendix.

9. Michael Poulos, *The Future of Banking: Six Trends that Will Shape the Industry*, Oliver Wyman, 9. www.oliverwyman.com/pdf_files/OW_EN_FS_2010_PUB_Future_of_Banking_LR.pdf

10. Patrick Jenkins, Brooke Masters, and Tom Braithwaite, "The Hunt for a Common Front," *Financial Times*, September 7, 2011.

11. Stephen Young, *Moral Capitalism: Reconciling Private Interest with the Public Good* (San Francisco: Berrett-Koehler Publishers, 2003), 58–59.

12. Ibid., 59.

13. Ibid., 58.

14. Jody Shenn and Michael J. Moore, "Goldman Grilled in Senate Hearing," *Bloomberg*, April 27, 2010, www.bloomberg.com/news/2010–04–27/goldman-execs-grilled-in-senate-hearing.html.

15. William D. Cohan, *Money and Power: How Goldman Sachs Came to Rule the World* (New York: Doubleday, 2011), 15–16.

16. Ibid., 16.

17. Ibid., 533.

18. *The Economist*, "The Goldman Hearings, Sachs and the Shitty: A Ghastly Day on Capitol Hill for Goldman Sachs' Top Brass," April 29, 2010.

19. Cohan, *Money and Power*, 19–20.

20. Bethany McLean and Joe Nocera, *All the Devils Are Here: The Hidden History of the Financial Crisis* (New York: Penguin/Portfolio, 2010), 362.

21. U.S. Securities and Exchange Commission, "Goldman Sachs to Pay Record $550 Million to Settle SEC Charges Related to Subprime Mortgage CDO," news release, Washington, D.C., July 15, 2010.

22. Goldman Sachs, "Report of the Business Standards Committee," January 2011, 2.

23. U.S. Securities and Exchange Commission, "Summary of Allegations," *Securities and Exchange Commission, Plaintiff, v. Reserve Management Company, Inc., Resrv Partners, Inc., Bruce Bent Sr., and Bruce Bent II, Defendants.* May 5, 2009, 2.

24. Ibid., 3.

25. Ginia Bellafante, "Gunning for Wall Street, With Faulty Aim," *New York Times*, September 23, 2011.

26. Andrew Ross Sorkin, "On Wall Street, a Protest Matures," *New York Times*, October 3, 2011.

27. Ibid.

28. HeardofEconomics, Forum Post: "Occupy Wall Street is Leaderless Resistance Movement with People of Many Colors, Genders, and Political Persuasions," Occupy Wall Street, October 18, 2011, http://occupywallst.org/forum/occupy-wall-street-is-leaderless-resistance-moveme/

29. Brad Plumer, "IMF: Income Inequality Is Bad for Economic Growth," *Wonkblog, Washington Post*, October 6, 2011, www.washingtonpost.com/blogs/ezra-klein/post/imf-income-inequality-is-bad-for-growth/2011/10/06/gIQAjYADQL_blog.html.

30. Bonnie Kavoussi, "Widening Income Inequality Bad for Economic Growth: IMF Report," *Huffington Post*, September 20, 2011, www.huffingtonpost.com/2011/09/20/income-inequality-economic-growth_n_969933.html.

31. Jeremy Grantham, "Quarterly Letter Part 2: Danger—Children at Play," quarterly newsletter published by GMO (August 2011), 5.

32. Ibid.

Chapter 3 Stewardship Defined: Feeding Your Flock First

1. The Holy Bible: *New International Version* (Colorado Springs, CO: Biblica, 2011).

2. Peter Block, *Stewardship: Choosing Service Over Self-Interest* (San Francisco: Berrett-Koehler Publishers, 1993), xx.

3. *Merriam-Webster Online Dictionary 2011*, s.v. "stewardship," www.merriam-webster.com/dictionary/stewardship.

4. Al Watts, *Navigating Integrity* (Minneapolis, MN: Brio Press, 2011), 128.

5. Block, *Stewardship*, 6.

6. Stephen Young, *Moral Capitalism: Reconciling Private Interest with the Public Good* (San Francisco: Berrett-Koehler, 2003), 3.

7. Ibid., 3, 6.

8. Larry Spears, *Reflections on Leadership: How Robert K. Greenleaf's Theory of Servant Leadership Influenced Today's Top Management Thinkers* (New York: John Wiley & Sons, 1995), 2.

9. Ibid., 3, 7.

10. Ibid., 4.

11. Young, *Moral Capitalism*, 59.

12. Ibid., 58.

13. Spears, *Reflections on Leadership*, 3.

14. Watts, *Navigating Integrity*, 68.

15. Ibid., 20.

16. Block, *Stewardship*, 41.

17. Doug Lennick and Fred Kiel, *Moral Intelligence 2.0: Enhancing Business Performance and Leadership Success in Turbulent Times* (Boston: Pearson Prentice Hall, 2011), xiv.

18. Paul Purcell, interview with author, September 23, 2011.

19. E. Stanley O'Neal, "Remarks" (opening convocation, Howard University, Washington, D.C., September 24, 2004).

20. Purcell interview.

21. Block, *Stewardship*, 18.

22. Young, *Moral Capitalism*, 54.

23. Ibid., 56.

24. Ibid., 56.

25. Watts, *Navigating Integrity*, 134.

26. Spears, *Reflections on Leadership*, 4.

27. Ibid.

28. Watts, *Navigating Integrity*, 134.

29. Arthur C. Parker, *The Constitution of the Five Nations or The Iroquois Book of the Great Law* (Albany, NY: University of the State of New York, 1916), 38–39.

30. John C. Bogle, *Enough: True Measures of Money, Business, and Life* (Hoboken, NJ: John Wiley & Sons, 2009), 117.

31. Young, *Moral Capitalism*, 49.

32. Doug Lennick and Fred Kiel, *Moral Intelligence: Enhancing Business Performance and Leadership Success* (Upper Saddle River, NJ: Wharton School Publishing, 2008), 7, 79.

33. Bill George, *Authentic Leadership: Rediscovering the Secrets to Creating Lasting Value* (San Francisco: Jossey-Bass, 2003), 1.

34. Charles D. Ellis, *The Partnership: The Making of Goldman Sachs* (New York: Penguin Press, 2008), xiv.

35. James B. Stewart, "At UBS, It's the Culture That's Rogue," *New York Times*, September 23, 2011.

36. Ibid.

37. Ibid.

38. Purcell interview.

Chapter 4 World's Safest Banking System: Canada, the New Switzerland

1. Royal Bank of Canada, "First Quarter 2011 Earnings Release," March 3, 2011, www.rbc.com/investorrelations/pdf/q111release.pdf.

2. Robert Wessel, interview with the author.

3. Chrystia Freeland, "What Toronto Can Teach New York and London," *Financial Times*, January 29, 2010.

4. Terry Campbell, "Our Banks: Safety and Soundness amid Global Uncertainty," Remarks for International Finance Club of Montreal, Canadian Bankers Association, October 27, 2011.

5. Chrystia Freeland, "What Toronto Can Teach New York and London."

6. Jaime Caruana and Anoop Singh, *Canada: Financial System Stability Assessment* (Washington, DC: International Monetary Fund and Capital Markets Department, 2008).

7. FDIC, "Failed Bank List," Updated December 1, 2011. www.fdic.gov/bank/individual/failed/banklist.html.

8. James F. Dingle, *Planning an Evolution: The Story of the Canadian Payments Association, 1980–2000, Bank of Canada and the Canadian Payments Association*, May 2003. This was a joint publication of the Bank of Canada and the Canadian Payments Association. Available at: www.bankofcanada.ca/wp-content/uploads/2010/07/dingle_book.pdf.

9. Thomson One; RBC Capital Markets.

10. Carol Ann Northcott, Graydon Paulin, and Mark White, "Lessons for Banking Reform: A Canadian Perspective," *Central Banking* 19, 4 no. 4 (May 20, 2009): 53n.

11. *Toronto Globe and Mail* Update, "2011 Rankings of Canada's Top 1000 Public Companies by Profit," June 23, 2011.

12. John Kiff, *Canadian Residential Mortgage Markets: Boring but Effective?* (Washington, DC: International Monetary Fund, Working Paper 09/130, Monetary Capital Markets, 2009), 4.

13. Canadian Bankers Association, "Number of Residential Mortgages in Arrears," as of September 2011, www.cba.ca/en/component/content/publication/69-statistics.

14. Kiff, *Canadian Residential Mortgage Markets*, 12.

15. Chrystia Freeland, "What Toronto Can Teach New York and London."

16. Ibid.

17. Erik Heinrich, "Why Canada's Banks Don't Need Help," *Time*, November 10, 2008.

18. Northcott, et al., "Lessons for Banking Reform: A Canadian Perspective," 49.

19. John Murray, "Canada and the Economic Crisis," 80th International Business Cycle Conference of the Kiel Institute, Berlin, Germany, September 2009, 15.

20. National Commission on the Causes of the Financial and Economic Crisis in the United States, *The Financial Crisis Inquiry Report*, p. xix.

21. Ibid., xx.

22. Lev Ratnovski and Rocco Huang, *Why Are Canadian Banks More Resilient?* (Washington, DC: International Monetary Fund, Working Paper 09/152, Western Hemisphere Department, 2009).

23. Robert Wessel, *The Canadian Banks "The End of an Era,"* Presentation to RBC Executive Team, June 2011, 11.

24. Andre Philippe-Hardy, *Canadian Bank Primer* 3rd ed., RBC Dominion Securities, August 2010, 21.

25. Lev Ratnovski and Rocco Huang, *Why Are Canadian Banks More Resilient?* 18.

26. Chrystia Freeland, "What Toronto Can Teach New York and London."

27. Ibid.

28. Chris Crosby (former RBC Chief Strategy Officer), in discussion with author.

29. Jeffrey Hollender and Linda Catling, *How to Make the World a Better Place* (New York: W. W. Norton & Company, 1995), 6.

30. Thelma Beam and Hugh Oddie. *Americans are from Mars, Canadians are from Venus*, presentation for Royal Bank of Canada. Canadian Cultural Research/ Odditie Inc. 2001.

Chapter 5   Making the System Stronger: In Defense of Dodd–Frank and Basel III

1. US SIF, "Social Investment Forum Commends Senate for Joining House of Representatives in Approving Financial Reform Bill," news release, July 15, 2010.

2. Tim Ryan, "Emerging Implications for the Economy, Clients and Your Business" (Opening remarks, SIFMA Regulatory Reform Summit: Dodd-Frank Impact Analysis, New York, July 13, 2011).

3. Timothy Geithner, "A Dodd-Frank Retreat Deserves a Veto," Opinion, *Wall Street Journal*, July 20, 2011.

4. Secretary Henry M. Paulson Jr., "U.S. Treasury Secretary's Blueprint for Regulatory Reform: Secretary Paulson's Plan to Improve Regulation of U.S. Financial Markets" (Remarks, U.S. Department of the Treasury, Washington, D.C., March 31, 2008).

5. Tom Lauricella and Peter A. McKay, "Dow Takes a Harrowing 1,010.14-Point Trip," *Wall Street Journal*, May 7, 2010.

6. Motoko Rich and Graham Bowley, "Markets Expected Credit Ruling, but Risks Remain, Analysts Say," *New York Times*, August 6, 2011.

7. *The Economist* Special Report, "Capital: How Much Is Enough?" *The Economist*, May 14, 2011.

8. Ibid., 11.

9. Markus Böhme, et al., "Day of Reckoning? New Regulation and Its Impact on Capital-Markets Businesses," *McKinsey & Company*, September 2011.

10. Satyajit Das, *Extreme Money* (Upper Saddle River, NJ: FT Press, 2011), 270.

11. "Dodd-Frank Progress Report," Davis Polk & Wardwell LLP, November 2011, 7.

12. SIFMA, "Outlook for the Financial Sector Summary," (Regulatory Reform Summit 2011, New York City, July 13, 2011).

13. Tim Ryan, Statement for the Record before the House Financial Services Committee, June 16, 2011.

14. Tim Ryan, "Seeking Clarity on Regulatory Coordination," *The Hill's Congress Blog*, April 12, 2011, http://thehill.com/blogs/congress-blog/lawmaker-news/155447-seeking-clarity-on-regulatory-coordination.

15. Morgan Stanley and Oliver Wyman, *Wholesale and Investment Banking Outlook*, March 23, 2011, 4.

16. Alan Greenspan, "Regulators Must Risk More, and Intervene Less," *The A-List* (blog), *Financial Times*, July 26, 2011.

17. Morgan Stanley and Oliver Wyman, *Wholesale and Investment Banking Outlook*, March 23, 2011, 1.

18. Philip Suttle, "The Cumulative Impact on the Global Economy of Changes in the Financial Regulatory Framework," *Institute of International Finance*, September 2011, 8.

19. Ibid.

20. Macroeconomic Assessment Group established by the Financial Stability Board and the Basel Committee on Banking Supervision, "Assessment of the Macroeconomic Impact of Higher Loss Absorbency for Global Systemically Important Banks," Bank for International Settlements, October 10, 2011.

21. Ben Protess, "Is Dodd-Frank Overdue or Overkill? 2 Dueling Views," *New York Times*, August 3, 2011.

22. Bill Johnstone, in discussion with author, October 5, 2011.

Chapter 6   Making the Investor Safer: In Defense of New Fiduciary Rules

1. Barbara Roper, "Fiduciary Duty: What Investors Need to Know," *Huffington Post*, August 30, 2010, www.huffingtonpost.com/barbara-roper/post_768_b_699447.html.

 2. Barbara Roper, September 26, 2011 (10:49 a.m.) comment on Mark Schoeff, Jr., "Fiduciary Timetable Pushed Back into 2012," *InvestmentNews*, September 25, 2011. www.investmentnews.com/article/20110925/REG/309259987.

 3. Julie Creswell, "Pressing All the Buttons for a Panic Attack," *New York Times*, August 7, 2011.

 4. Chas Burkhart, in discussion with the author, October 5, 2011.

Chapter 7   To Investors Standing on the Wings: Prepare for the Next Crisis

1. Nassim Nicholas Taleb, *The Black Swan: The Impact of the Highly Improbable* (New York: Random House, 2007), xviii, xxviii.

 2. Ibid., 136.

 3. Ibid., 157.

 4. Ibid., 203.

 5. Ibid., xxi.

 6. Ibid., 225.

 7. Barton Biggs, *Wealth, War, and Wisdom* (Hoboken, NJ: John Wiley & Sons, 2008), 323.

 8. Ibid., 321.

 9. Ibid., 332.

10. See Appendix C.

11. Jeremy Grantham, *Reinvesting When Terrified*, quarterly newsletter published by GMO, March 2009.

12. For more information, see: Andrew F. Krepinevich, *7 Deadly Scenarios: A Military Futurist Explores War in the 21st Century* (New York: Bantam Dell, 2009).

13. Biggs, *Wealth, War, and Wisdom*, 326.

14. Taleb, *Black Swan*, xix.

15. James Montier, "The Seven Immutable Laws of Investing," GMO, March 11, 2011.

16. Warren Buffett, "Berkshire Hathaway Shareholder Letter 2008," 3.

17. Warren Buffett, "Berkshire Hathaway Shareholder Letter 2010," 22, 24.

18. Berkshire Hathaway, "2008 Annual Report," Berkshire Hathaway, Inc., 29.

19. Michael Poulus, "The Future of Banking: Six Trends that Will Shape the Industry," Oliver Wyman, 2010, 9, Exhibit 2.

20. James Montier, "The Seven Immutable Laws of Investing."

21. Biggs, *Wealth, War and Wisdom*, 332.

22. Ibid., 320.

23. Jeremy Grantham, "Letters to the Investment Committee XVII, Part 2: On the Importance of Asset Class Bubbles for Value Investors and Why They Occur," quarterly newsletter published by GMO (January 2011).

24. Chesley B. Sullenberger III, *Highest Duty: My Search for What Really Matters* (New York: HarperCollins, 2009).

25. Jason Zweig, "Too Flustered to Trade: A Portrait of the Angry Investor," The Intelligent Investor, *Wall Street Journal*, August 20, 2011.

26. Jim Cramer, "Machines Are Driving Out Small Investors," *The New Real Money*, August 12, 2011, http://realmoney.thestreet.com/articles/08/12/2011/machines-are-driving-out-small-investors.

27. Lee Brodie, "High Frequency Traders Manipulating the Nasty Sell-Off?" CNBC.com, August 8, 2011, www.cnbc.com/id/44035012/High_Frequency_Traders_Manipulating_the_Nasty_Sell_Off.

28. John F. Wasik, "Beat High-Frequency Trading Machines by Not Playing Their Game," *Reuters Money* (blog), Reuters, August 29, 2011, http://blogs.reuters.com/reuters-money/2011/08/29/beat-high-frequency-trading-machines-by-not-playing-their-game/.

29. Phil Dow, "Monthly Market Commentary: Predatory Volatility," *RBC Capital Markets*, September 2011.

30. Graham Bowley, "Clamping Down on Rapid Trades in Stock Market," *New York Times*, October 8, 2011.

Chapter 8   Environmental, Social, and Governance Investing: Could It Be the Answer?

1. Jeffrey Hollender and Linda Catling, *How to Make the World a Better Place: 116 Ways You Can Make a Difference* (New York: W.W. Norton, 1995), xix.

2. Stephen Young, *Moral Capitalism: Reconciling Private Interest with the Public Good* (San Francisco: Berrett-Koehler, 2003), 8, 47.

3. John C. Harrington, *Investing with Your Conscience: How to Achieve High Returns Using Socially Responsible Investing* (New York: John Wiley & Sons, 1992).

4. Social Investment Forum Foundation, "Report on Socially Responsible Investing Trends in the United States 2010," 14.

5. Amy Domini, "Want to Make a Difference? Invest Responsibly," *The Huffington Post*, March 14, 2011, www.huffingtonpost.com/amy-domini/want-to-make-a-difference_b_834756.html.

6. Joseph F. Keefe, "Sustainable Investing and the Next Economy" (speech to the Boston Economic Club, Federal Reserve Bank of Boston, June 15, 2010).

7. Who Cares Win, "Future Proof? Embedding Environmental, Social and Governance Issues in Investment Markets; Outcomes of the Who Cares Wins Initiative 2004–2008," International Finance Corporation, Swiss Federation, and the UN Global Compact, 3–4; and author.

8. Asset Management Working Group of the United Nations Environment Programme Finance Initiative and Mercer, "Demystifying Responsible Investment Performance: A Review of Key Academic and Broker Research on ESG Factors," October 2007, 50.

9. Laura Gitman, Blythe Chorn, and Betsy Fargo, "ESG in the Mainstream: The Role for Companies and Investors in ESG Integration," BSR, September 2009, 12–13.

10. United Nations PRI, "Commitment of Investors to Responsible Investing Continues to Grow," September 7, 2011. www.unpri.org/press/2011%20RoP%20press%20release.pdf.

11. United Nations PRI, "The Principles for Responsible Investment," www.unpri.org/principles/

12. Ibid.

13. Imogen Rose-Smith, "Doing Well, Doing Good," *Institutional Investor*, November 2010, 82.

14. Ibid.

15. Anthony Ling, et al., "Introducing GS SUSTAIN," Goldman Sachs, June 22, 2007, 1.

16. Ibid., 8.

17. Ibid., 1.

18. Thao Hua, "Search for ESG Alpha Continues," *Pensions & Investments*, January 24, 2011.

19. Ibid.

20. Chris McKnett, et al., *Sustainable Investing: Positioning for Long-Term Success* (Boston: State Street Global Advisors, October 2010), 5.

21. Thao Hua, "ESG Gains Wider Acceptance," *Pensions & Investments*, January 24, 2011.

22. Social Investment Forum Foundation, "Report on Socially Responsible Investing Trends in the United States 2010," 8.

23. McKnett, et al., *Sustainable Investing*, 3.

24. Yvon Chouinard, Jib Ellison, and Rick Ridgeway, "The Big Idea: The Sustainable Economy," *Harvard Business Review*, October 2011, 6.

25. Gordon Nixon, "Navigating the Gray Area: The State of Responsible Investing" (speech, RBC Dexia Investor Services Conference, May 24, 2007).

26. *Harvard Business Review*, "Spotlight: The Good Company," November 2011, 66–65.

27. McKnett, et al., *Sustainable Investing*, 4.

28. UN PRI news release, "New Data Signals Growing 'Culture Change' Amongst Significant Portion of Global Investors," July 16, 2009.

29. McKnett, et al., *Sustainable Investing*, 4.

30. Blythe Chorn, et al., "ESG in the Mainstream," *BSR*, 6.

31. Chouinard, Ellison, and Ridgeway, "The Big Idea."

32. Tom Van Dyck, interview with the author, July 25, 2011.

33. Imogen Rose-Smith, "Doing Well, Doing Good," *Institutional Investor*, November 2010, 82.

34. Joseph F. Keefe, "Sustainable Investing and the Next Economy" (speech to the Boston Economic Club, Federal Reserve Bank of Boston, June 15, 2010).

35. Ibid.

36. Sheila Bonini and Steph Görner, "The Business of Sustainability: McKinsey Global Survey Results," *McKinsey Quarterly*, October 2011.

37. Vikram Pandit/Charlie Rose Interview at SIFMA Annual Meeting, November 8, 2011.

38. Chouinard, Ellison, and Ridgeway, "The Big Idea," 5.

39. Who Cares Win, *Future Proof? Embedding Environmental, Social and Governance Issues in Investment Markets; Outcomes of the Who Cares Wins Initiative 2004–2008*,

International Finance Corporation, Swiss Federation, and the UN Global Compact, 3–4.

40. Ibid., 4.

41. Steven Pearlstein, "Wall Street's Mania for Short-Term Results Hurts Economy," *Washington Post*, September 11, 2009.

42. Aspen Institute Business & Society Program, "Overcoming Short-Termism: A Call for a More Responsible Approach to Investment and Business Management," September 9, 2009, 3.

43. Ibid., 2.

44. James Montier, *Was It All Just A Bad Dream? Or, Ten Lessons Not Learnt*, white paper, GMO (February 2010), 6.

Chapter 9   Communities, Caring, and Commitment: Reconnecting with Our Stewardship Responsibilities

1. Joseph F. Keefe, "Sustainable Investing and the Next Economy" (speech to the Boston Economic Club, Federal Reserve Bank of Boston, June 15, 2010).

2. "The Road to a Downgrade," *Wall Street Journal*, July 28, 2011, http://on.wsj.com/pgyTjl.

3. William H. Gross, "Investment Outlook: Rocking-Horse Winner," PIMCO.com, April 2010, http://europe.pimco.com/EN/Insights/Pages/Rocking-Horse%20Winner%20April%202010%20IO.aspx.

4. Setting and Meeting an Appropriate Target for Fiscal Sustainability: Hearing Before the Senate Budget Committee (statement of Rudolph G. Penner, "Choosing the Nation's Fiscal Future," February 11, 2010).

5. Ibid.

6. *The Economist*, "Substandard & Poor," August 13, 2011.

7. *The Economist*, "Looking for Someone to Blame," August 13, 2011.

8. *The Economist*, "Fighting for its Life: Euro Zone Is in Intensive Care," *The Economist*, September 17, 2011.

9. Wolfgang Schäuble, "Why Austerity Is Only Cure for the Eurozone," *Financial Times*, September 5, 2011.

10. Jonathan Burton, "Grantham: 'No Market for Young Men'" *MarketWatch*, September 21, 2011.

11. *The Economist*, "Be Afraid," October 1, 2011.

12. *The Economist*, "Welcome to the Anthropocene," May 26, 2011.

13. Jeremy Grantham, "Time to Wake Up: Days of Abundant Resources and Falling Prices Are Over Forever," quarterly newsletter published by GMO (April 2011), summary.

14. Ibid., 2.

15. Thomas L. Friedman, "The Fat Lady Has Sung," *New York Times*, February 21, 2010.

16. Grantham, "Time to Wake Up," 8.

17. Jeremy Grantham, "Resource Limitations 2: Separating the Dangerous from the Merely Serious," quarterly newsletter published by GMO (July 2011), 2.

18. Ibid., 3.

19. Financial Crisis Inquiry Commission, "The Financial Crisis Inquiry Report," January 2011, xvii.

20. Bill George, *Authentic Leadership: Rediscovering the Secrets to Creating Lasting Value* (San Francisco: Jossey-Bass, 2003), 2.

21. Ibid., 5.

22. Michael Lewis and David Einhorn, "The End of the Financial World As We Know It," *New York Times*, January 4, 2009.

23. Michael Lewis, *Boomerang: Travels in the New Third World* (New York: W.W. Norton 2011), 202.

24. Ibid.

25. Ibid.

26. Henri J. M. Nouwen, "January 23: Community, A Quality of the Heart," in *Bread for the Journey: A Daybook of Wisdom and Faith* (San Francisco: Harper-Collins, 1997).

27. Doug Lennick and Fred Kiel, *Moral Intelligence 2.0: Enhancing Business Performance and Leadership Success in Turbulent Times* (Boston: Pearson Prentice Hall, 2011), 47.

28. C. S. Lewis, *The Screwtape Letters* (New York: Harper and Brothers, 1942), 77.

Glossary of Selected Financial and Regulatory Reform Terminology*

asset-backed securities   A bond–like instrument backed by a pool of financial claims such as loans, leases, credit card receivables, installment contracts, and just about any other contractually defined stream of payments (other than payments from real estate securities). Like any fixed–income security, the investor is paid an interest rate. These figured prominently in the financial crisis because they are examples of a type of financing known as *securitization* (see further on), which enabled financial institutions to book fees for originating the loans, leases, and receivables; book fees for structuring the securities; and then sell off most of the securities, thus dumping the residual risk or any responsibility on the borrowers.

*SOURCE: Some definitions drawn from Campbell R. Harvey's Hypertextual Financial Glossary, available for iPad/iPhone at http://bit.ly/hfgplus.

assets under management The total market value of assets that an investment advisor manages on behalf of its clients. Frequently used as a measure of a financial institution's size.

bank leverage The amount of borrowed money banks have on their balance sheets.

Basel III The third version of a multinational bank regulatory framework agreed upon by 27 countries on September 12, 2010. The name for the accords is derived from Basel, Switzerland, where the Basel Committee on Banking Supervision, the entity that issues the accords, meets. The goal of Basel III is to make the global financial system safer, sounder, more stable, and more secure than it was before the financial crisis. On a good day, the complexity of Basel requirements will give anyone a headache. And there are more regulatory entities with fingers in the Basel pie than there are characters in a Tolstoy novel. See Chapter 5 and Appendix B for a more complete description of Basel reforms.

capital ratios Various measures of the financial health of banks.

capital requirements Regulations that require banks and other financial institutions to back their assets with a set amount of equity capital to maintain a strong balance sheet. The purpose is to ensure healthy institutions that can protect deposits, withstand shocks, and avoid default even under extreme market conditions.

Commodity Futures Trading Commission (CFTC) An independent agency with a mission to regulate commodity futures and options markets in the United States.

common equity Also called *common stock*. Holders of these securities are a company's owners. Common equity is a security in the capital structure of a company. In the event of a firm's liquidation, common equity holders are paid last, after bondholders, preferred shareholders, and other debt holders.

Consumer Financial Protection Bureau (CFPB) Agency established by the Dodd-Frank Act of 2010 to protect consumers by carrying out federal consumer financial laws.

credit default swaps A credit derivative contract between two parties in which the buyer makes periodic payments (over the term of the contract to the seller, in exchange for a commitment to receive a set payment if a third party defaults. Generally used as insurance against default but also used for speculation. These were perhaps foremost in Warren Buffett's mind when he described derivative securities as "financial weapons of mass destruction."

debt restructuring   The process of modifying the terms of a loan to provide financial relief to the holder of the loan, whether it be an individual or a company. The purpose is for the debtor to avoid default. The restructuring may include extending the period of repayment, reducing the total amount owed, or exchanging a portion of the debt for equity in the debtor's company.

default   The failure to make a timely payment of interest or principal on a debt security, or to otherwise comply with the provisions of a bond indenture. A nonpayment default usually involves the breach of a covenant.

Department of the Treasury   The executive agency responsible for advising the president on economic and financial issues and fostering improved governance in financial institutions. It collects taxes, creates currency, manages government accounts and the public debt, supervises national banks and thrift institutions, and prosecutes tax evaders, among other duties.

depository institutions   Financial institutions that fund themselves primarily by taking deposits from the public. This includes commercial banks, savings and loan associations, savings banks, and credit unions. Deposits are viewed as a relatively (though not always) stable and low-risk source of funding. In the world of Basel III reforms, the ability of financial institutions to attract deposits has become increasingly valuable.

deregulation   A decrease in the power of regulators and the number and scope of government regulations. Deregulation means a reduction in the role of government in commerce and markets.

derivatives   A financial contract whose value is based on, or derived, from an underlying, more traditional security such as a stock or bond or commodity, or a market index, such as a stock market or interest rate index.

diversification   Investing strategy that calls for "not putting all your eggs in one basket," but for allocating investment funds among a variety of asset classes from conservative to risky, from stocks, to bonds, to real estate to gold, so as to minimize risk. As capital markets become more global and interdependent, diversification appears to be losing its ability to reduce volatility during periods of extreme volatility. At least, that was the experience of investors during the last financial crisis, as described in Chapter 6.

Dow Jones Industrial Average   Called "the Dow" for short, the best-known U.S. index of U.S. stocks. A price-weighted average of 30 actively traded blue-chip stocks, including stocks that trade on the New York Stock Exchange. The Dow is a barometer of how shares of the largest U.S. companies are performing.

environmental, social, and governance (ESG) investing   Environmental, social, and governance investing is the latest evolution of what is generally referred to as socially responsible investing (SRI). Also called impact investing, and sustainable investing, ESG investing looks to the corporate responsibility practices of corporations for indications of how companies, and their stock prices, will perform over long time periods.

exchange-traded funds (ETFs)   Similar to index mutual funds in the sense that their underlying portfolios are not generally (or at least didn't used to be) actively managed. These securities differ from index funds, however, in that their stocks trade continuously on exchanges (thus the name). Two popular ETFs are the Standard and Poor's Depositary Receipt (SPDR), launched in 1993, and the NASDAQ-100 Index Tracking Stock (QQQ), which was launched in 1999. These vehicles are popular for hedging as well as for gaining low-cost exposure to both broad and narrow asset classes and to specific sectors of the equity markets. In an example of how just about any product innovation can be used in the wrong way, the use of ETFs by certain types of traders has recently been blamed for increased volatility in the equity markets.

Federal Deposit Insurance Corporation (FDIC)   An independent agency created by by the Glass-Steagall Act of 1933. The FDIC provides deposit insurance up to $250,000 per individual depositor. The FDIC also examines and supervises banking institutions for safety and soundness and manages the liquidation of failed banks.

Federal Housing Finance Agency (FHFA)   Created on July 30, 2008, when the president signed into law the Housing and Economic Recovery Act of 2008. It provides effective supervision, regulation, and housing mission oversight of Fannie Mae, Freddie Mac, and the Federal Home Loan Banks to promote their safety and soundness, support housing finance and affordable housing, and support a stable and liquid mortgage market.

Federal Reserve Board   Established in 1913, the U.S. central bank's mission is to set monetary policy and to supervise financial services holding companies and certain banks.

Federal Trade Commission (FTC)   A U.S. government agency established in 1914 that promotes consumer protection and enforces laws aimed at preventing anticompetitive business practices.

fiduciary duty   For many, the client protection equivalent of the Holy Grail. It generally refers to the responsibility of an advisor in charge of the assets or affairs of a client to put their clients' interests first, without regard to their own interests. It sounds ideal. But like the Holy Grail, it doesn't exist in the form people think it exists. There is no one universal definition of what it means to be a fiduciary. The concept of fiduciary duty has been defined in different ways by different state laws. Precedent has been built up over many years by court rulings in cases that generally claim that a fiduciary's duty has been breached. At the federal level, the word *fiduciary* is defined in the Employee Retirement Income Security Act (ERISA), but nowhere else. As described in Chapter 5, it is a key element of the Dodd–Frank Act.

Financial Stability Oversight Council (FSOC)   Will provide comprehensive monitoring to ensure the stability of the U.S. financial system. The Council is charged with identifying threats to the financial stability of the United States, promoting market discipline, and responding to emerging risks to the stability of the United States' financial system.

Financial Industry Regulatory Authority (FINRA)   The largest independent regulator for all securities firms doing business in the United States. FINRA's mission is to protect America's investors by making sure the securities industry operates fairly and honestly. All told,

FINRA oversees nearly 4,460 brokerage firms, about 160,485 branch offices, and approximately 629,520 registered securities representatives.

full-recourse loans   No matter what risk event occurs, the borrower guarantees to repay this type of debt.

futures contract   A contract to buy or sell a particular commodity or financial product at a predetermined price in the future, such as a crude oil futures contract.

futures market   A market in which futures contracts are bought and sold, such as the Chicago Mercantile Exchange (CME).

G-20   The Group of Twenty was established in 1999 in the wake of the 1997 "Asian Contagion" financial crisis to bring together major advanced and emerging economies with the goal of stabilizing the global financial market. The G-20 is made up of the finance ministers and central bank governors of 19 countries plus the European Union: Argentina, Australia, Brazil, Canada, China, France, Germany, India, Indonesia, Italy, Japan, Mexico, Russia, Saudi Arabia, South Africa, Republic of Korea, Turkey, the United Kingdom, and the United States of America. The European Union is the 20th member of the G-20.

global capital requirements   Basel III rules that determine the amount of capital that banks and financial institutions must hold. These requirements are intended to apply and to be enforced consistently across national borders.

global equity markets   The various individual stock markets of the countries of the world in various time zones, from the United States to the United Kingdom to China to Brazil.

Government Accountability Office   An arm of the U.S. Congress established in 1921 to improve the performance and accountability of the federal government by investigating, evaluating, and auditing various government agencies and programs. Headed by the Comptroller General of the United States.

hedge fund   An investment fund, usually (but not always) structured as a private investment partnership, that manages a portfolio of investments using various strategies. Hedge funds come in so many shapes and sizes that the term is almost meaningless without further descriptors. Generally, however, a hedge fund serves as a vehicle for active managers to manage their clients' money with as few constraints and restrictions as possible, so as to maximize their ability to generate positive returns (also known as absolute returns) under all market conditions. Hedge fund managers often earn an annual fee (as much as 2 percent of assets under management) and a percentage of any profits they earn for their investors. These profits are sometimes calculated on the basis of their clients' original investment. Sometimes, profits are calculated as anything earned over and above a hurdle rate (such as the rate of interest clients could have earned on U.S. Treasury securities). Hedge funds fall into a category of investment opportunities called *alternative investments*, or, more specifically, *liquid alternatives*.

leverage ratio   The face amount of a firm's debt in relation to the total assets or equity of the firm. One basic measure of financial soundness.

liquidity   In the context of securities, a high level of trading activity, allowing buying and selling with minimum price disturbance. Liquid markets are characterized by the ability to buy and sell with relative ease. In the context of a financial institution, the ability of the institution to meet its short-term obligations. One of the concerns with getting regulatory reform right is to ensure that new rules do not reduce market liquidity. Also, most observers feel the Basel Committee has a lot more work to do to come up with new liquidity rules that are workable.

loan loss reserves   Funds set aside as a cushion to cover future losses from impaired and defaulted loans.

mortgage-backed securities   The root of all evil in Western civilization, if you read the library of books about the financial crisis. They are a type of asset-backed security in which the source of repayment and the collateral are underlying mortgage loans on residential or commercial real estate. The mortgage finance market in the United States changed over the last several decades from one in which banks held the loans on their balance sheets (an "originate-to-hold" model, which still prevails in countries like Canada) to one in which banks packaged the loans and sold them to third-party investors (an "originate-to-sell" model). The Dodd-Frank Act will force lenders to keep more skin in the game by requiring them to retain up to 5 percent of the risk in loan pools.

These are the targets of new authority given to the Commodity Futures Trading Commission by the Dodd-Frank Act.

Municipal Securities Rulemaking Board (MSRB)   Established by Congress in 1975 as a self-regulatory organization that protects investors and the public interest by promoting a fair and efficient municipal securities market. It includes the protection of state and local government issuers, public pension plans, and others whose credit stands behind municipal bonds, in addition to protecting investors and the public interest.

new equity issue or initial public offering (IPO)   Securities offered to the public for the first time through the issuance and listing of shares, in a company whose equity had previously been held by a restricted group of people.

off-balance-sheet activities (OBS)   Financing that is not shown as a liability on a company's balance sheet. OBS activities can be used by company management to mislead shareholders and hide a company's riskier activities.

Office of Financial Research (OFR)   Housed within the Treasury Department. Will support the FSOC and its member agencies by providing them with better financial data, information, and analysis so that policy makers and market participants have a more complete understanding of risk in the financial system. Created by the Dodd-Frank Act in 2010.

Office of the Comptroller of the Currency (OCC)   Independent bureau within the Department of Treasury that charters, regulates, and supervises all national banks and certain branches and agencies of foreign banks in the United States.

over-the-counter derivatives   A type of financial derivative that has its transaction directly negotiated between two parties rather than through an exchange. Some financial derivatives, such as a swap, a forward rate agreement, or an exotic option, are usually done over the counter.

private equity funds   Originally called leveraged buyout funds, these are financial firms such as KKR & Co. L.P. and the Blackstone Group L.P. These private equity firms often buy public companies using large amounts of debt, take them private, re-engineer the management, and then take them public again, earning a management fee for themselves and hopefully a return for their investors.

proprietary trading   Principal trading in which a firm seeks to profit for its own account, rather than execute a transaction for a client and earn a commission or other transaction fee. This activity will be significantly prescribed by a provision in the Dodd-Frank Act known as the Volcker Rule (after former Federal Reserve chairman Paul Volcker). Trying to define what activities constitute proprietary trading, as opposed to market making on behalf of clients and asset-liability management by financial institutions, is proving to be extremely difficult. Proposed regulations implementing Volcker provisions are extraordinarily complex, opaque, confusing, and open-ended. At this early stage of their development, they represent more a cry for help from regulators than a workable blueprint for reform.

regulatory arbitrage   The legal practice of financial firms migrating to other geographic markets to take advantage of more—favorable regulatory regimes—for example, a U.S. hedge fund setting up shop in the Cayman Islands because of less onerous regulations. It also refers to activities, employees, and investors moving from highly regulated organizations (such as banks) to more lightly regulated organizations (for example, hedge funds).

regulatory infrastructure   The overall matrix of various entities and rules that governs financial institutions and financial markets in the United States and globally.

retail deposits   Monies deposited at banks by individuals, as opposed to corporations. Often called core deposits, because they tend to be relatively stable from a financial institution's point of view. (See *depository institutions*.)

return on equity (ROE)   An indicator of profitability. Determined by dividing net income by total common stockholder equity. The result is shown as a percentage. Investors use ROE as a measure of how effectively a company is using shareholders' money.

risk-weighted capital   Requirement that banks hold a minimum ratio of their estimated total capital to their estimated assets, based on how risky those assets are.

Securities and Exchange Commission (SEC)   An independent federal agency with a mission to protect investors; maintain fair, orderly, and efficient securities markets; and facilitate capital formation.

securitization   A funding technique whereby banks and investment banks create complex securities that pool the future cash flows from a variety of assets such as loans, leases, credit card receivables, installment contracts, and residential and commercial mortgages. (See *asset-backed securities* and *mortgage-backed securities*.)

shadow banking system   Consists of lightly regulated financial entities like hedge funds and sovereign wealth funds that until now fell outside of the authority of the SEC, the Fed, and other regulators.

socially responsible investing   See *ESG investing*.

sovereign wealth fund   State-owned entities that operate with varying degrees of transparency as portfolio managers for the wealth of individual nations whose wealth is derived from quite a diverse range of sources. Sovereign wealth funds have become increasingly important players in the global financial markets over the past decade. Examples include China Investment Corporation, Government Pension Fund of Norway, Canada Alberta Heritage Fund, Qatar Investment Authority, Ireland's National Pensions Reserve Fund, and the Australia's Future Fund.

Standard & Poor's 500 Index   Index of 500 widely held common stocks that is a proxy for the general performance of the largest companies in the U.S. stock market on a market capitalization basis.

subprime mortgage   Mortgages that are issued to people who are not by traditional standards qualified to repay them. These mortgages are often issued in the expectation that the homeowner's income will rise in the future. In periods of weakness in the housing market or the economy, people with subprime mortgages are the first to default.

suitability standard   A requirement for advisors who work for brokerage firms that any investing strategy they recommend to a client is suitable for that client, given their overall circumstances, including their age, net worth, previous investment experience, risk tolerance, and investment objectives. Quickly being replaced by a fiduciary standard.

systemic risk The possibility that the financial system experiences a massive disruption due to its interconnectedness and complexity, which would ultimately harm all markets and asset classes.

Troubled Asset Relief Program (TARP) TARP began in October 2008 as a vehicle for the U.S. Treasury to buy illiquid assets from banks and other financial institutions, which allowed these institutions to stabilize their balance sheets. TARP was introduced in the wake of the U.S. subprime mortgage crisis.

wholesale funding Sources of funds that banks use in addition to retail bank deposits to finance their operations and manage risk. Wholesale funding sources include Federal Reserve funds, third-party debt, preferred stock, securitization, and brokered deposits. Wholesale funds are generally viewed as less stable and reliable than retail deposits.

Author's Guide to Supplemental Readings

In my effort to better understand recent events, I made it a habit to read virtually everything that was written about the financial crisis. Here is my highly subjective guide to some of the more important crisis books.

Understanding the Financial Crisis

Too Big to Fail: The Inside Story of How Wall Street and Washington Fought to Save the Financial System—and Themselves by Andrew Ross Sorkin (Penguin, 2009)

Start here, with this, which is the gold standard in retrospective narratives about the financial crisis. Fast-paced and comprehensive, it's got all the key players, both people and institutions. Really the only "who-did-what-to-whom-when" book you'll need to read.

The Big Short by Michael Lewis (W.W. Norton & Company, 2010)

By far the most entertaining book about the crisis. In classic Lewis style, it is a deliciously witty character study of a handful of misfit personalities eccentric enough to have deconstructed and bet against the entire developed world's multitrillion-dollar system of housing finance. Leading the cast: a corporate-lawyer-turned-contrarian-analyst so confrontational even his wife describes him as "sincerely rude," Steve Eisman. Then there is Michael Burry, an ex-doctor with Asperger's syndrome and a glass eye whose investors vilified him and demanded their money back only a few months before he doubled the value of their investments.

Boomerang: Travels in the New Third World by Michael Lewis (W.W. Norton & Company, 2011)

Michael Lewis strikes again. Although not the most polished of Lewis's books, it nonetheless offers the first overview of the fiscal insanity that has brought European nations to the same precipice that global financial institutions faced in 2008 and 2009. Lewis describes the investment hypothesis of one hedge fund manager. Sovereign nations, crippled by the entitlement promises they've made to their citizens compounded their fiscal stress by rescuing their banks. In doing so, nations have created the very real possibility that their inability to pay their debts may plunge the world into another global financial crisis. Lewis also develops the notion that the causes of the crises we are facing go beyond mere leadership failure to "a problem with the entire society . . . of people taking what they can, just because they can, without regard to the larger social consequences," and captures this perfectly with his image of men and women "alone in a dark room with a pile of money."

On the Brink: Inside the Race to Stop the Collapse of the Global Financial System by Henry M. Paulson (Business Plus, 2010)

The ultimate insider's account of the U.S. government's bailout of the financial system, from its chief architect, salesman, and implementer . . . President George Bush's Treasury secretary. Often making it up on the fly, Paulson made a lot of mistakes. But he and his colleague, Federal Reserve chairman Ben Bernanke, deserve the Congressional Medal of Honor for saving the United States, and perhaps other G-7 countries, from a second Great Depression.

The Financial Crisis Inquiry Report by the Financial Crisis Inquiry
  Commission (PublicAffairs, 2011)
  At some point, you'll need to eat your lima beans and digest at least
the executive summary of this, the official account of the financial
crisis.

Morals and Ethics in Business Leadership

Moral Capitalism: Reconciling Private Interest with the Public Good by
  Stephen Young (Berrett-Koehler, 2003)
  Maybe because he's a Midwesterner (St. Paul, Minnesota–based
former dean of Hamline Law School), I find Young's recipe for restoring
capitalism as a force for good (*moral capitalism* as opposed to *brute capi-*
talism) to be refreshingly clear-eyed, straightforward, and practical.

Moral Intelligence: Enhancing Business Performance and Leadership Success
  (Pearson Prentice Hall, 2008) and *Moral Intelligence 2.0: Enhancing*
  Business Performance and Leadership Success in Turbulent Times (Pearson
  Prentice Hall, 2011) by Doug Lennick and Fred Kiel
  More straightforward and understandable wisdom from Mid-
westerners, this time from a veteran of IDS, a Minneapolis-based
diversified financial institution. What is it in the water here, which is
drawn from the Mississippi River? A call to action for corporate leaders
to do the right thing based on the premise that ". . . altruistic and
cooperative behavior is part of basic human behavior today because it
was crucial to the survival of our early ancestors. . . ."

Enough: True Measures of Money, Business, and Life by John C. Bogle
  (John Wiley & Sons, 2009)
  The "conscience of Wall Street" often sounds like a scold, but
his observation that for "many of the wealthiest and most powerful
among us, there seems to be no limit today on what *enough* entails"
is powerful and worth reflecting on. "Not knowing what *enough* is
subverts our . . . values. . . . It makes salespersons of those who
should be fiduciaries. . . . [T]his . . . leads us astray in our larger lives.
We chase the false rabbits of success; we too often bow down at the
altar of the transitory and . . . meaningless and fail to cherish what
is . . . eternal."

Authentic Leadership: Rediscovering the Secrets to Creating Lasting Value by
Bill George (Jossey-Bass, 2003).

Guess where he's from—yep, Minneapolis again. Like Robert
Greenleaf, who created the concept of servant leadership, the former
chairman and CEO of Medtronic has embarked on a second career as a
commentator on the attributes of effective leadership. He has become
a resource for CEOs looking to raise the bar when it comes to the
value they add inside and outside the workplace.

Individual Investing

Wealth, War, & Wisdom by Barton Biggs (John Wiley & Sons 2008)

A historical account of which asset classes and wealth preservation
strategies worked best during World War II, a period of social and
economic disruption many times greater than what we experienced in
2008 and 2009. Includes a world-class collection of Winston Churchill
stories and sayings. A double bonus for history buffs: Biggs's ideal asset
allocation plan is based on his World War II research: 60 percent
stocks, 30 percent bonds, 5 percent real assets and 5 percent in assets
held abroad. The ideal wealth preservation strategy: "Anticipate the
anticipation of trouble." (See Taleb, next.)

The Black Swan by Nassim Nicholas Taleb (Random House, 2007)

If arrogance were a virtue, Taleb would be a living saint. But his
central premise ranks up there in importance with that of Alcoholics
Anonymous: Grant me wisdom to know that reality is random, and
that I cannot foresee, predict, prevent, or avoid precisely those
occurrences and events that will affect me the most. All we can do is to
position ourselves for the unpredictable.

*Pioneering Portfolio Management: An Unconventional Approach to Institu-
tional Investment* by David F. Swensen (Free Press, 2009)

I didn't quote from Swensen's book in *Stewardship*. And he
declined to let me interview him . . . so I confess to being a bit miffed.
Nonetheless . . . this description of the role and purpose of different
asset classes and investment strategies by the chief investment officer of
the Yale endowment is a classic. Intelligence on parade. But, as they

say, "Don't try this at home." What works for Yale doesn't work for most individual investors. Or most institutional investors, for that matter.

Winning the Loser's Game by Charles D. Ellis (5th ed. McGraw-Hill, 2009)

This is the first book I read upon entering the investment management business. And along with Swensen's, it is still one of the best. The notion that "time is Archimedes' lever" in investing, that investment strategies need to be aligned with and driven by the investor's time horizon, that winning by not losing should be the goal of most individual investors—those are seminal principles that can save many people from a lot of emotional stress during the periods of extreme volatility we seem to be experiencing these days in global capital markets.

Quarterly Newsletters by Jeremy Grantham

Run, do not walk, to register (www.gmo.com) for and become a regular reader of Grantham's quarterly commentaries on whatever he thinks is compellingly important at the time. For example, several recent issues have been devoted to what he believes may be a paradigm shift in the price of the scarce commodities on which the human race depends for survival, and on which economies depend for continued growth. From the single most intelligent investor practicing today. Grantham believes passionately in "regression to the mean" and that "the only thing that matters in investing are [sic] the bubbles and the busts." Grantham's firm, Grantham, Mayo, Van Otterloo & Co. (GMO) is the only money manager I know to publish, and to update quarterly, forecasts of the returns on various asset classes (in GMO's case, over a seven-year horizon). GMO's forecasts have proven uncannily accurate and prescient.

Additional Sources

Ackerman, Andrew. "SEC Targets 'Abacus' Deals." *Wall Street Journal*, September 20, 2011.

Ackerman, Andrew. "Shapiro Still Sees Fissures in Financial System." *Wall Street Journal*, June 21, 2011.

Adam, Shamim. "El-Erian: World on Eve of Next Financial Crisis." *Bloomberg*, September 22, 2011.

Andrews, Suzanne. "The Woman Who Knew Too Much." *Vanity Fair*, November 2011.

Bachus, Spencer, and Jeb Hensarling. "One Year Later: The Consequences of the Dodd-Frank Act." Washington, DC: Financial Services Committee.

Barton, Dominic. "Capitalism for the Long Term." *Harvard Business Review*, March 1, 2011.

Bernstein, Donald S., et al. "Client Memorandum: FDIC's Second Notice of Proposed Rulemaking under the Orderly Liquidation Authority." Davis Polk & Wardwell LLP, March 28, 2011.

Biggs, Barton. "No More Water, the Fire Next Time." *Macroeconomic Thoughts*, August 10, 2011.

Blinder, Alan S. "Two Cheers for the New Bank Capital Standards." *Wall Street Journal*, September 20, 2010.

Bloomberg News. "SEC Wants Money Funds to Buffer Up: Sources." *InvestmentNews*, August 2, 2011.

Bolli, Agathe, and Gianreto Gamboni. "Education Note: Socially Responsible Investing." *UBS Wealth Management Research*, December 10, 2007.

Braithwaite, Tom, and Patrick Jenkins. "JPMorgan Chief Says Bank Rules 'Anti-US.'" *Financial Times*, September 12, 2011.

Bruni, Frank. "Humble Service with a Side of Swag." *New York Times Sunday*, August 21, 2011.

Burstein, Katherine, and Craig Metrick. "DC Plan Management and Pension Inconsistency: Is Your Plan at Risk?" Mercer, 2010.

Burton, Jonathan. "Grantham: 'No Market for Young Men.'" *MarketWatch*, September 21, 2011.

Carver, Laurie. "Excessive Capital Requirements Will Make Markets More Chaotic—Myron Scholes." *Risk Magazine*, June 22, 2011.

Cheng, Beiting, Ioannis Ioannou, and George Serafeim. "Corporate Social Responsibility and Access to Finance, Working Paper 11–130." Harvard Business School, May 18, 2011.

Cohan, William D. "Lehman's Demise, Dissected." *New York Times*, March 18, 2010.

Credit Suisse. "Global Equity Strategy: Andrew Garthwaite and Team, US Morning Call." Credit Suisse Securities (Europe), September 13, 2011.

Cui, Carolyn. "For Money Managers, a Smarter Approach to Social Responsibility." *Wall Street Journal*, November 5, 2007.

Dallas, George. "REO Viewpoint: Banking As If the Economy Mattered." F&C Investments, October 2011.

Donlan, Thomas G. "Charitable Contribution: The MacArthur Foundation Funds a Timely Reminder of Fiscal Imprudence." *Barron's*, January 18, 2010.

Dow Jones. "RBC's Nixon Frustrated by Basel III Rules." *American Banker*, September 20, 2011.

The Economist. "America's Downgrade: Substandard & Poor," August 13, 2011.

The Economist. "America's Bail-Out Maths: Hard-Nosed Socialists," June 11, 2011.

The Economist. "Dimon Geezer," July 16, 2011.

The Economist. "Don't Blame Canada: A Country that Got Things Right," May 14, 2009.

The Economist. "Europe's Currency Crisis: How to Save the Euro," September 17, 2011.

The Economist. "Goldman Sachs and the SEC: Greedy Until Proven Guilty," April 22, 2010.

The Economist. "Investing During a Crisis: Nowhere to Hide," October 15, 2011.

The Economist. "Investment Banking: The Big Squeeze," February 19, 2011.

The Economist. "The Euro-Zone Crisis: Fighting for Its Life," September 17, 2011.

The Economist. "The Goldilocks Recovery: Strict Financial Regulation and a New Commodity Boom Have Turned 'Boring' Canada into an Economic Star," May 6, 2010.

The Economist. "The Proper Diagnosis: Profligacy Is Not the Problem," September 17, 2011.

Eder, Steve, Michael Rothfeld, and Aaron Lucheti. "Probe into Goldman Widens." *Wall Street Journal,* September 7, 2011.

Einhorn, David, and Michael Lewis. "Jan. 4, 2009: Wall Street's Fatal Blind Spot." *New York Times,* September 25, 2010.

Ellison, Jib, et al. "When Nature Gets Valued," Blu Skye Sustainability Consulting, May 14, 2010.

Epstein, Gene. "Corporate Tax Hurdles: A World of Difference." *Barron's,* April 18, 2011.

Farrell, Paul B. "Goldman's Secret Moral Pathology." *MarketWatch,* November 24, 2009.

Fidler, Stephen. "The Next Step for Europe: Putting Its Plan to the Test." *Wall Street Journal,* October 28, 2011.

Freeland, Chrystia. "Canada's Great Escape." *Financial Times,* January 30, 2010.

Freeman, James. "The Weekend Interview with Paul Singer: Mega-Banks and the Next Financial Crisis." *Wall Street Journal,* March 19, 2011.

French, Kristen. "The *New* New Deal." *Registered Rep.,* April 1, 2011.

Friedman, Thomas L. "The Clash of Generations." *New York Times,* July 17, 2011.

Friedman, Thomas L. "When Economics Meets Politics." *New York Times,* February 3, 2010.

Grantham, Jeremy. "Feet of Clay: Alan Greenspan's Contribution to the Great American Equity Bubble." *GMO Special Topic Paper,* October 2002.

Grantham, Jeremy. "Immoral Hazard." *GMO Quarterly Letter,* April 2008.

Gross, Bill. "Warning to Washington: Don't Mess with the Debt Ceiling." *Washington Post,* July 13, 2011.

Haanaes, Knut, et al. "Sustainability: The 'Embracers' Seize Advantage." *MIT Sloan Management Review* and Boston Consulting Group, Research Report Winter 2011.

Hall, Kevin G. "Few Foreclosures, No Bank Failures: Canada Offers Lessons." *McClatchy Newspapers,* July 12, 2011.

Harwood, John. "Spend Now, Save Later, Bond Fund Leaders Say." *New York Times,* August 22, 2011.

Jenkins, Holman W. Jr. "The Weekend Interview with James Grant: The Scourge of the Faith-Based Paper Dollar." *Wall Street Journal*, July 17, 2011.

Jenkins, Patrick. "Failure to Tackle Lessons from 2008." *Financial Times*, September 12, 2011.

Jenkins, Patrick. "No More Agreement over What to Do about Banks." *Financial Times*, September 12, 2011.

Kanter, Rosabeth Moss. "What Would Peter Say?" *Harvard Business Review*, November 2009.

Karnitschnig, Matthew. "Cheers and Skepticism Greet European Deal: Dow Jumps 339.51 Despite Questions." *Wall Street Journal*, October 28, 2011.

Kopecki, Dawn. "Dimon Asks If Bernanke Shares 'Fear' of Rules Slowing Economic Recovery." *Bloomberg*, June 7, 2011.

Kramer, Mark R., and Michael E. Porter. "Creating Shared Value." *Harvard Business Review*, January 2011.

Kramer, Mark R., and Michael E. Porter. "Strategy and Society: The Link Between Competitive Advantage and Corporate Social Responsibility." *Harvard Business Review*, December 2006.

Lauricella, Tom. "Pivot Point: Investors Lose Faith in Stocks." *Wall Street Journal*, September 26, 2011.

Lohr, Steve. "First, Make Money. Also, Do Good." *New York Times*, August 14, 2011.

Lonon, Yasmine, and Laura Nishikawa. "Industry Report—North America: Continued Exposure to Sustainability Challenges." *MSCI ESG Research*, March 2011.

Mattingly, Phil. "FDIC Approves 'Living Wills' Rule for Largest Bank Failures." *Bloomberg*, September 13, 2011.

McTague, Tim. "A Not-So-Happy Birthday for Dodd-Frank." *Barron's*, July 4, 2011.

Mendonca, Lenny T., and Jeremy Oppenheim. "Investing in Sustainability: An Interview with Al Gore and David Blood." *The McKinsey Quarterly*. Web exclusive, May 2007, www.mckinseyquarterly.com/Investing_in_sustainability_ An_interview_with_Al_Gore_and_David_Blood_2005.

Morgenson, Gretchen. "Suddenly, Over There Is Over Here." *New York Times*, September 17, 2011.

Nishikawa, Laura. "Thematic Report: Global Banks, ESG Risk in the Global Banking Sector." RiskMetrics Group, June 2010.

Nishikawa, Laura. "Which Banks Create the Most Social Utility for the Least Systemic Risk?" MSCI ESG Research, 2011.

Nixon, Simon. "ICB Takes Shot at Bank-Heavy Britain." *Wall Street Journal*, September 13, 2011.

Nonaka, Ikujiro, and Hirotaka Takeuchi. "The Big Idea: The Wise Leader." *Harvard Business Review*, May 2011.

Norton, Leslie P. "The Dangers of Lessons Unheeded." *Barron's*, March 21, 2011.

O'Donohoe, Nick, Christina Leijonhufvud, and Yasemin Saltuk. *Impact Investments: An Emerging Asset Class*. J.P. Morgan Global Research, prepared in partnership with the Rockefeller Foundation and the Global Impact Investing Network. November 29, 2010. Available at: www.jpmorgan.com/pages/jpmorgan/investbk/research/impactinvestments.

Philbrick, Nathaniel. "The Road to Melville." Adapted from "Why Read Moby Dick?" *Vanity Fair*, November 2011.

Porter, Tony. "Canadian Banks in the Financial and Economic Crisis." McMaster University, Hamilton, Canada. Paper prepared for presentation at the Policy Responses to Unfettered Finance Workshop, North-South Institute, Ottawa, Canada, June 8–9, 2010.

Prahalad, C. K. "The Responsible Manager." *Harvard Business Review*, January 2010.

Protess, Ben. "Court Ruling Offers Path for Challenging Dodd-Frank Rules." *New York Times*, August 18, 2011.

Rappaport, Liz. "Banks Hit For Credit Union Ills." *Wall Street Journal*, March 23, 2011.

RBC Wealth Management. "Market Update: Looking Beyond the S&P downgrade." Global Portfolio Advisory Committee, August 8, 2011.

Reiner, Karen. "Most Environmentally and Socially Controversial Companies of 2010." *RepRisk*, December 15, 2010.

Rich, Frank. "The Bipartisanship Racket." *New York Times*, December 19, 2010.

Rotella, Carlo. "Can Jeremy Grantham Profit from Ecological Mayhem?" *New York Times*, August 11, 2011.

Sanchez, Gloria. "The Educational Foundation of America." Brandes Investment Partners, September 20, 2011.

Schoeff Jr., Mark. "Dodd-Frank: As a Rule, the Going Has Been Slow." *InvestmentNews*, July 17, 2011.

Seib, Gerald F. "Voters' Faith Deficit Widens." *Wall Street Journal*, May 25, 2010.

SIFMA. "SIFMA CEO Testifies on Impact of Dodd-Frank Regulations on Jobs and U.S. Competitiveness." June 16, 2011, www.sifma.org/news/news.aspx?id=25991.

SIFMA. "Systemic Risk Information Study." *SIFMA*, June 2010.

Simon, Ruth, and Nick Timiraos. "What Did Fannie, Freddie Know?" *Wall Street Journal*, September 6, 2011.

Solomon, Deborah. "FDIC's Bair: New Capital Rules Won't Hurt Lending." *Wall Street Journal*, June 10, 2011.

Steinert-Threlkeld, Tom. "SIFMA's Ryan: Capital Surcharge a Threat to U.S. Competitiveness." *Securities Technology Monitor*, September 6, 2011.

Story, Louise, and Gretchen Morgenson. "For Goldman, A Deal's Stakes Keep Growing." *New York Times*, April 17, 2010.

Strasburg, Jenny, and Jean Eaglesham. "Subpoenas Go Out to High-Speed Trade Firms." *Wall Street Journal*, August 8, 2011.

Surowiecki, James. "The Goldman Hearings: Levin vs. Wall Street." *New Yorker*, April 27, 2010.

Taibbi, Matt. "The Great American Bubble Machine." *Rolling Stone*, April 5, 2010.

Taibbi, Matt. "Why Isn't Wall Street in Jail?" *Rolling Stone*, February 16, 2011.

Tarullo, Daniel K. "Regulating Systemically Important Financial Firms." Speech at the Peter G. Peterson Institute for International Economics, Washington, D.C. Federal Reserve, June 3, 2011.

Tedesco, Theresa. "The Great Solvent North." *New York Times*, February 28, 2009.

Tett, Gillian. "Beware a Hegelian Touch of Regulatory Hubris." *Financial Times*, September 14, 2011.

Tett, Gillian. "In the Dock, but Not in Jail." *Financial Times*, March 11, 2011.

Thomas, Bill, Keith Hennessey, and Douglas Holtz-Eakin. "What Caused the Financial Crisis?" *Wall Street Journal*, January 27, 2011.

Torres, Craig, and Cheyenne Hopkins. "Fed Said to Track Basel Capital Rules for Biggest U.S. Banks." *Bloomberg*, August 11, 2011.

U.S. Department of the Treasury. "Remarks by Treasury Secretary Tim Geithner to the International Monetary Conference." Atlanta, Georgia, June 6, 2011.

United Nations Environment Programme. "Fiduciary Responsibility." A report by the Asset Management Working Group of the UNEP Finance Initiative, July 2009.

Wall Street Journal. "Everyone Bails Out Everyone," October 28, 2011.

Wall Street Journal. "So Much for the Volcker Rule," October 24, 2011.

Warren, Elizabeth. "Wall Street's Race to the Bottom," February 8, 2010.

Zakaria, Fareed. "Worthwhile Canadian Initiative." *Newsweek*, February 7, 2009.

Acknowledgments

I never would have been able to write this book without the help and support of three people. My agent and editor, Leah Spiro, who provided me a framework for and the confidence to expand early chapters into a book and who helped shape my weekend fragments into a more coherent whole. Sally Schreiber, my intern, who competently handled the never-ending list of administrative details that surround a project like this. And my wife, Laura, who encouraged me to search for the Stewardship message I have been experimenting with for many years and who helped me find the voice with which to say what I wanted to say. I am grateful to Pamela van Giessen, Evan Burton, and Emilie Herman at John Wiley & Sons, who recognized the timeliness and relevance of the big idea of Stewardship and took a chance on me; to my friends and industry colleagues who agreed to be interviewed: Chas Burkhart, Charley Ellis, Bill Johnstone, Paul Purcell, Jeff Slocum, Tom Van Dyck, and Brian Walsh; to Tim Ryan and the management team at SIFMA—Ken Bentsen, Ira Hammerman, Randy Snook, Cheryl

Crispen, Ileane Rosenthal, John Maurello, and David Krasner—who provided me with a ringside seat at the Dodd-Frank regulatory reform table; and to my colleagues at RBC, George Lewis, Jim Little, Katherine Gay, and Lynne Patterson, who supported this effort and gave me the freedom, rare for someone in my position and role, to write a book while running a wealth management firm.

About the Author

J ohn Taft is CEO of RBC Wealth Management in the United States, one of America's largest full-service retail brokerage firms. The firm has approximately 2,000 financial advisors in 42 states with 200 offices, and $220 billion in assets under administration. It is owned by RBC, the Royal Bank of Canada, a $65 billion institution based in Toronto.

In 2011, John served as chairman of the Securities Industry and Financial Markets Association (SIFMA), the leading securities industry trade group representing securities firms, banks, and asset managers in the United States. John led SIFMA during the debate and implementation of major financial reform legislation, the Dodd-Frank Act, and has testified before Congress in support of a federal fiduciary standard of care for investment professionals who provide advice to individual clients.

John has worked in the financial services business since 1981, serving as: chairman, president and CEO of Voyageur Asset Management; president and CEO of Dougherty Summit Securities; a member of the board of directors of Segall, Bryant and Hamill, the Clifton Group, and Vintage Mutual Funds; and as a managing director at Piper,

Jaffray & Hopwood. John was also assistant to the mayor of the City of St. Paul, Minnesota. He began his career as a journalist.

An active advocate of diversity, John serves as executive sponsor for RBC Wealth Management's Gay, Lesbian, Allied and Diverse Employees (GLADE) employee resource organization. Under his leadership, RBC Wealth Management has received a rating of 100 percent in the Human Rights Campaign's Corporate Equality Index. In 2010, John was named the "Outstanding Corporate Diversity Leader" by the National Gay & Lesbian Chamber of Commerce (NGLCC).

John has served in a variety of roles at a wide range of not-for-profit and public-service organizations. They include: Walker Art Center, Macalaster College, Breck School, Northwest Area Foundation, Minnesota Public Radio, Twin Cities Public Television, St. Paul Chamber Orchestra, Minnesota Film Board, Illusion Theater and Minnesota Film Board, and the Itasca Group. He has served on the Mayor's Council on Economic Development Finance, Blue Ribbon Commission on Pensions, and the Mayor's Working Group on Local Government Finance.

John has appeared on CNBC, Fox, Fox Business News, Bloomberg TV, thestreet.com, and FT.com, and has been published in the *New York Times*, *National Journal*, *Parade* magazine, the *New Republic*, the *Real Paper*, *Taos News*, *Santa Fe New Mexican*, *Minneapolis Star Tribune*, and the *St. Paul Pioneer Press*. John is a frequent presenter and speaker at various events across the country, including the Securities Industry Institute at the Wharton School and the Center for Ethical Business Cultures at the University of St. Thomas in Minneapolis.

John graduated magna cum laude, Phi Beta Kappa, with a bachelor of arts degree from Yale University in New Haven, Connecticut, and earned a master's degree in public and private management from the Yale School of Organization and Management.

John and his wife, Laura, live in Minneapolis and Montreal. He has three children, Mary Allison, Lauren, and Colin, and two step-children, Gabrielle and Liam.

Index